Interactive Videoconferencing

K–12 Lessons That Work

Edited by

Kecia Ray

Jan Zanetis

International Society for Technology in Education
EUGENE, OREGON • WASHINGTON, DC

Interactive Videoconferencing
K–12 Lessons That Work

Edited by Kecia Ray and Jan Zanetis

Director of Book Publishing: *Courtney Burkholder*
Acquisitions Editor: *Jeff V. Bolkan*
Production Editors: *Lynda Gansel, Lanier Brandau*
Production Coordinator: *Rachel Bannister*
Graphic Designer: *Signe Landin*
Rights and Permissions Administrator: *Lanier Brandau*
Copy Editor: *Nancy Olson*
Cover Design, Book Design and Production: *Kim McGovern*

Library of Congress Cataloging-in-Publication Data

Ray, Kecia.
  Interactive videoconferencing : K-12 lessons that work / Kecia Ray, Jan Zanetis. — 1st ed.
    p. cm.
  Includes bibliographical references.
  ISBN 978-1-56484-251-0 (pbk.)
  1. Teleconferencing in education. 2. Videoconferencing. I. Zanetis, Jan. II. Title.
  LB1044.9.T38R39 2009
  371.3'58—dc22

                                               2008053538

First Edition
ISBN: 978-1-56484-251-0

Printed in the United States of America

International Society for Technology in Education (ISTE)
Washington, DC, Office:
    1710 Rhode Island Ave. NW, Suite 900, Washington, DC 20036-3132
Eugene, Oregon, Office:
    180 West 8th Ave., Suite 300, Eugene, OR 97401-2916
Order Desk: 1.800.336.5191
Order Fax: 1.541.302.3778
Customer Service: orders@iste.org
Book Publishing: books@iste.org
Rights and Permissions: permissions@iste.org
Web: www.iste.org

About ISTE

The International Society for Technology in Education (ISTE) is the trusted source for professional development, knowledge generation, advocacy, and leadership for innovation. A nonprofit membership association, ISTE provides leadership and service to improve teaching, learning, and school leadership by advancing the effective use of technology in PK–12 and teacher education.

Home of the National Educational Technology Standards (NETS), the Center for Applied Research in Educational Technology (CARET), and the National Educational Computing Conference (NECC), ISTE represents more than 85,000 professionals worldwide. We support our members with information, networking opportunities, and guidance as they face the challenge of transforming education. To find out more about these and other ISTE initiatives, visit our website at **www.iste.org**.

As part of our mission, ISTE Book Publishing works with experienced educators to develop and produce practical resources for classroom teachers, teacher educators, and technology leaders. Every manuscript we select for publication is carefully peer-reviewed and professionally edited. We look for content that emphasizes the effective use of technology where it can make a difference—increasing the productivity of teachers and administrators; helping students with unique learning styles, abilities, or backgrounds; collecting and using data for decision making at the school and district levels; and creating dynamic, project-based learning environments that engage 21st-century learners. We value your feedback on this book and other ISTE products. E-mail us at **books@iste.org**.

About the Authors

Kecia Ray

Kecia Campbell-Ray began her career as a middle school science teacher in Dekalb County, Georgia. She taught in one of the first 21st-Century classrooms in the state of Tennessee. Dr. Ray conducted research in technology literacy assessment as an Assistant Professor at Middle Tennessee State University before being invited to develop the technology design for Frist Center for the Visual Arts. In 2000, she became the Director of Technology Research in the Office of Science Outreach at Vanderbilt University School of Medicine.

Dr. Ray is a member of the International Society for Technology in Education (ISTE) where she is the elected Vice President of the Telecom Special Interest Group. She is an invited member of the North American Council for Online Learning Research Committee and an invited Commissioner with the Montessori Accreditation Council for Teacher Education. She has conducted research in the area of technology integration across the U.S., and in Canada and South Africa. She is an author of books and articles focused on teaching through technology and consults with school systems, universities, and museums designing learning networks. Dr. Ray presents nationally and internationally and serves as adjunct professor in the College of Natural and Applied Sciences at Lipscomb University as well as graduate faculty for the college of Teaching and Learning at University of Maryland University College. She currently serves as the Assistant Superintendent of Federal Programs and Grants for Metropolitan Nashville Public Schools, Tennessee, where she oversees district policy and planning, administration of federal and categorical grants, family and community engagement, and professional development. She resides in Nashville with her husband, Dr. Clark Ray.

Jan Zanetis

Jan taught special education (K–6) and regular education (7–8) for 20 years after obtaining her Bachelor's degree from Vanderbilt University and her Master's degree from Tennessee State University. In her final years in the classroom, she was a science teacher and recognized as a "21st Century" teacher. In 2000, she returned to her alma mater and served as the Director of the Vanderbilt Virtual School. Using the resources of the faculty and staff, she developed hundreds of standards-based lessons for K–12 students across the U.S., using videoconferencing as the main means of delivery. In 2005, Jan became the Global Market Manager for Education at TANDBERG, the world leader in video-conferencing solutions. TANDBERG is a proud member of the ISTE 100. Jan has been an active ISTE member over the years, serving on various NECC committees, contributing to *L&L*, and recently served as a presenter in the ISTE Webinar series. She currently serves as the President of SIG-IVC. Jan is also active on committees within CoSN, Internet2, the Center for Interactive Learning and Collaboration (CILC), and has most recently joined the Board of Directors of the United States Distance Learning Association.

We would like to thank our families for their support and encouragement during the writing of this book.

Contents

Preface

Do not confine your children to your own learning,
for they were born in another time.
—HEBREW PROVERB

A fundamental goal for educational technology is for technology to be transparent. That is to say that when teachers appropriately integrate technology into their classrooms, no one notices. What parents do notice is the enthusiasm in their children's voices when they describe a story written at school using Inspiration software. They notice a child's excitement for science after an hour spent on the Internet looking up information about grasshoppers. Technology offers interaction to a classroom, and not with just teachers and classmates, but with people, places, and things beyond the walls of the classroom.

The How People Learn report from the National Research Council (2002) indicates that "the field of learning...needs to become more integrated in focus and draw together relevant fields for interdisciplinary collaborations" (p. 278). *Interactive Videoconferencing: K–12 Lessons That Work* is designed to help you break down the walls of your classroom and build interdisciplinary collaborations by integrating interactive videoconferencing (IVC) into your standards-based lessons. Specifically, this book focuses on a blend of interactive technologies that increase learning by building virtual classrooms.

We begin by introducing you to the digital-age student and providing research-based, yet practical, pedagogical practices. Then we share with you a collection of lessons that use collaborative technology and are organized by grade level and discipline. The lessons incorporate evaluation tools, student work samples, and guiding templates to help you get started.

We hope this book will become a valuable tool as you become an interactive classroom teacher. We also hope it will provide you some guidance for developing technology-rich interactive lessons without the stress of keeping up with the technology. Our book *Videoconferencing for K–12 Classrooms, Second Edition* (Cole, Ray, & Zanetis, 2009) outlines how classrooms should be physically constructed to facilitate videoconferencing. *Interactive Videoconferencing* focuses on management of your classroom and curriculum in an effort to put these interactive technologies into practice.

Chapter 1

Introduction

The Case for Interactive Classrooms

Technology has transformed modern society and is slowly transforming the modern classroom. When technology was first introduced in schools in the 1980s, it was expected to revolutionize the classroom structure. Alan November explained in his book *Empowering Students with Technology* (2001) that we are at the "beginning of a cultural shift toward collaboration and learning empowerment" where global learning allows students to construct genuine relationships across the globe. The shift moves us from a classroom isolated from the outside world to one collaborating with it. The introduction of technology into the classroom makes this possible. Technology empowers students to construct their own knowledge and become more motivated and engaged (Pflaum, 2004).

Throughout America, schools spend millions of dollars enhancing classrooms with technology, but inequities exist from district to district. Some districts have more funding than others and thus have a better opportunity to grow technology-rich programs. Some districts have the advantage of technology staff development and IT support that isn't available in other districts. Although some studies validate that technology enhances student performance, there have been no conclusive studies indicating a direct correlation, but much-needed funding wanes in those districts where lawmakers assess the impact that technology has on learning and find it wanting. Therefore, the focus in the classroom is on how teachers use technology as an instructional tool, and how they integrate technology into their existing curriculum so that students can learn how to use technology to enhance their learning.

Of course, just having computers, software, and various other forms of technology in our classrooms does not guarantee student success. This comes only when teachers are effective in the way they integrate these tools into teaching their subject matter. No Child Left Behind requires teachers to be highly qualified, but that does not necessarily mean highly effective. Highly effective teachers plan instruction and assessment based on anticipated student outcomes and student interests. Teachers must begin to listen to the needs of their students and understand student culture.

Some states have already begun to listen to their students. Virginia, New Mexico, Louisiana, Idaho, West Virginia, Arkansas, Georgia, and Pennsylvania are examples of states that have developed statewide, technology-rich programs to address student needs in an effort to increase student achievement. The programs are so successful that they are outlined in the National Technology Plan (U.S. Department of Education, 2004). Other states have taken notice of the impact interactive videoconferencing has on closing the achievement gap and are establishing statewide video networks.

Wyoming uses their video network to deliver AP and dual enrollment courses as well as enrichment and credit recovery programs (Marcel, 2004). South Dakota introduced the Center for Statewide E-learning at Northern State University in 2001 to provide service to K–12 schools and professional development for e-learning and instructional strategies (p. 12). North Dakota began their transformation in 1999 with legislation that mandated a statewide communications network (STAGEnet) that also supports K–12 instructional programming. Oregon was not far behind with the Oregon Access Network launched in 2001, providing 293 high schools with IVC (p. 15). In 2005, the Arkansas Legislature provided the funding to establish the K–12 Distance Learning Initiative. As a result of this legislation, the Arkansas Department of Education was able to install distance-learning equipment in the majority of Arkansas high schools, build a video network, and employ distance-learning specialists across the state.

The changes in society and the classroom due to technological advances have occurred so rapidly that teachers have struggled to keep up. Many teachers want to use technology in the classroom, but it changes at such a rapid rate that training of the teachers is not keeping up. Teacher preparation and professional development play a significant role in ensuring that teachers integrate technology properly, and the National Research Council (2001) reports that the ultimate measure of success for any teacher or professional development program is how well the students of these teachers learn after the teacher has received training. Professional development in technology integration is critical for teachers to become comfortable using technology as an instructional tool.

The National Technology Plan acknowledged the lack of adequate training and included a powerful recommendation to "tear down those walls" (U.S. Department of Education, 2004). The plan was constructed through interviews with students, parents, and teachers in addition to other significant stakeholders. A new term, *millennials*, was introduced to identify students who had grown up using digital information and communication technologies. The report indicated that the largest group of new Internet surfers was 2–5 years of age (p. 17).

Because younger students are entering school with advanced technology skills, teachers should be more prepared to use technology as an instructional tool at all levels. The fact that we do not embrace technology as a teaching tool causes students who enter school with high enthusiasm and keen technological literacy skills to become disenchanted with the education process at an early age. As part of the plan, students in Grades 3–6 were interviewed, and they expressed that they would like to use laptops not only to do everything in class but also to increase multimedia experiences. High school students wanted more virtual opportunities as well.

We know that when teachers engage students' auditory, visual, and kinesthetic senses, students become fully engaged in learning. This is exactly why many students love video games. Video games are visually tantalizing, with great sound effects, and require students to manipulate joysticks or buttons to direct the characters. These same facets may be incorporated into most lessons to make them more interactive. The more interaction that occurs within a lesson, the more likely all learning styles will be addressed.

Thinking outside of the traditional teaching-method box will be the key to effective teaching in the 21st century. Today's students no longer respond to sitting at desks in 45-minute intervals but, rather, prefer a more constructivist and project-based approach to learning. With more teachers trained in the constructivist model, we are doing a better job of covering our material in a more student-driven, collaborative, multisensory approach. Many teachers are encouraging students to use technology tools such as handheld devices and the computer to collect, analyze, and synthesize information and solve learning problems.

Videoconferencing and the Internet are two technologies that significantly build the level of interactivity in any lesson. Videoconferencing allows for visual and voice interaction beyond the walls of the classroom, while the Internet connects students to current information and provides a shared location for data. Developing web 2.0 lessons that include these two technologies guarantees increased interaction and enthusiasm in your classroom.

Interactive lessons involve more planning than your typical content lesson. The infusion of technology adds another dimension to the planning process. However, the payoff should be increased by student motivation. Students will also experience a more contextual understanding of the content when activities are used to prepare students for the IVC.

Planning the Interactive Lesson

Students should be well prepared for the videoconference. Lessons that use IVC as an instructional tool should have three distinct parts: pre-conference, videoconference, and post-conference. The pre-conference activity should prepare students for the content or collaboration to take place during the videoconference. This would include familiarizing students with vocabulary words, introducing concepts related to the content to be presented, and sharing the anticipated evaluation of the lesson. Students should also be aware of the videoconference schedule or agenda as well. If the videoconference is with a content provider, students should prepare some questions in advance. Students participating in a collaborative project should e-mail the far site to discuss expectations of the collaboration, and they should share any documents that may be referred to during the videoconference.

For interactive lessons to be successful, certain ground rules must be established for classroom instruction. Content delivered via videoconference is only as engaging as the student's willingness to actively participate during the session. Encouraging students to participate means that you will need to explain the rules of engagement prior to the IVC. Just as you instruct students not to talk when the teacher is talking and to raise their hands to speak, practices must be in place in the interactive classroom that will yield success. For instance, during a videoconference lesson, students should not block the view of the camera. Moving around the classroom is acceptable if the lesson dictates, but putting a hand over the camera lens or "unmuting" the mute button on the microphone without permission is never acceptable behavior. Likewise, students need to be taught how to search on the Internet so that the time they spend online is productive and beneficial to their research. So-called search coaches may be assigned to students who struggle to narrow down their keywords or have difficulty identifying valuable web sources.

IVC lessons may include

- project-based learning: coordinating projects by selecting real-world problems to research, using resources beyond the school or even local community;

- experiential learning: connecting through IVC with knowledge experts who engage students in activities related to developing that knowledge base;

- collaboration: partnering with a school in another state or country to collaborate on various projects or lessons;

- competency-based learning: connecting with specialists in a specific area, assessing knowledge before IVC and after to measure gains;

- integration: using IVC as a virtual textbook, as appropriate for the content and the lesson;

- learner-centered environment: allowing students to select program providers that interest them or empowering students to plan and implement their own content lesson for other students;

- communities of learning: establishing relationships with schools in other states or countries, sharing resources and learning experiences; and

- cognitive apprenticeship: using IVC as a tool for coaching and mentoring opportunities.

The planning of an IVC lesson should focus on the objective and student outcomes, just as any other lesson. The difference is ensuring that the technology will work and having a backup plan if it doesn't. Again, IVC lessons should always begin with a pre-conference activity and be followed up with a post-conference activity. Post-conference activities should include an evaluation that assesses comprehension of the delivered content or outcome of the collaboration.

Classroom applications of IVC can be broken down into four main categories, as outlined in the pyramid shown in the figure on the following page. The relative size of the category on the pyramid is reflective of:

1. the proliferation of this type of application, and

2. the historical emergence of the application.

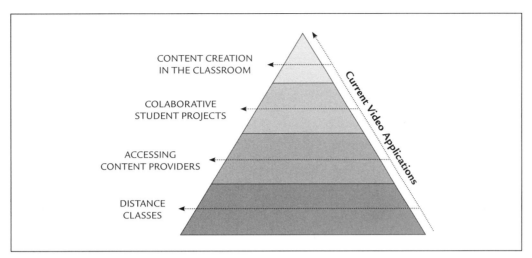

Categories of IVC applications

We will indicate the category that the lesson plans typify by using the pyramid indicator at the beginning of each lesson. Some lessons may combine two categories.

Beyond the use of videoconferencing in the classroom, online collaborative tools are readily available and accessible in schools. Using web 2.0 tools for collaborative classrooms offers students the opportunity to explore online learning in a familiar environment before entering the world of courseware. Teaching and modeling virtual collaborations prepares students to more purposefully use online tools while building information literacy. ISTE's NETS for Students stress the significance of student collaborations.

Designing interactive learning environments requires preparation on behalf of the teacher, but the payoff is great when students are fully engaged and enthusiastic about a lesson they may otherwise ignore. Beyond the enthusiasm, students are focused less on rote learning and more on problem solving that involves the use of many technologies students are exposed to in a global society (Davis & Edyburn, 2007).

Online collaborative student project lessons teach students how to work with other students and allow students to demonstrate their strengths while recognizing weaknesses. These collaborative environments enable students to encounter learning experiences beyond that which they would have had within the confines of a classroom and introduce them to worlds beyond their classroom walls. Starting students with web 2.0 applications such as student-created wikis or blogs, then escalating to IVC, takes collaboration to a whole new level. Those students they are connecting with in cyberspace suddenly have a face and personality!

The lessons in this book were created and tested by experienced classroom teachers from across the United States. Some lessons include samples of pre-conference and post-conference activities, while other lessons define student collaborative projects using videoconferencing. Lessons may use IVC content that requires a fee, but we encourage you to look at ways these lessons might be integrated into your classroom and your budget. Additionally, several free IVC resources are available to educators. Check out national IVC e-mail lists, ISTE's special interest groups SigIVC, or SigTel for more information about distance learning in K–12. These resources are outlined in Chapter 5.

Chapter 2

Elementary Lessons

Reading and Language Arts
Writer's Workshop with the United Kingdom

Mathematics
100th Day of School

Science
Awesome Insects: Scram, Squash, or Study?

Social Studies
Impacting Local History

Writer's Workshop with the United Kingdom

JOAN VAUGHAN, First-Grade Teacher
Waverly School, Eastchester, New York

JOHN BLASER, Technology Integration Specialist
Eastchester UFSD, Eastchester, New York

TYPE OF LESSON:	*Collaborative Project*
GRADE LEVEL:	*1–3*

The Evolution of Video Applications in Distance Education

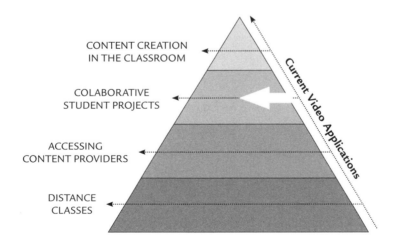

CONTENT CREATION IN THE CLASSROOM

COLABORATIVE STUDENT PROJECTS

ACCESSING CONTENT PROVIDERS

DISTANCE CLASSES

Current Video Applications

CORRELATION TO STANDARDS

Standards for the English Language Arts

NL-ENG.K-12.4 Communication Skills

Students adjust their use of spoken, written, and visual language (e.g., conventions, style, vocabulary) to communicate effectively with a variety of audiences and for different purposes.

NL-ENG.K-12.5 Communication Strategies

Students employ a wide range of strategies as they write and use different writing process elements appropriately to communicate with different audiences for a variety of purposes.

NL-Eng.K-12.6 Applying Knowledge

Students apply knowledge of language structure, language conventions (e.g., spelling and punctuation), media techniques, figurative language, and genre to create, critique, and discuss print and nonprint texts.

NL-Eng. K-12.12 Applying Language Skills

Students use spoken, written, and visual language to accomplish their own purposes (e.g., for learning, enjoyment, persuasion, and the exchange of information).

Reprinted with permission. © 1996 by the International Reading Association and the National Council of Teachers of English. Available at www.ncte.org/standards/.

UNIT GOALS

* To be able to integrate technology into our Writer's Workshop.

* To provide opportunities for students to work together as a committee and experience peer teaching.

LESSON OBJECTIVES

After completing this lesson, students will be able to

* read, write, listen, and speak for information and understanding;

* read, write, listen, and speak for literary response and expression;

* read, write, listen, and speak for critical analysis and evaluation;

* read, write, listen, and speak for social interaction;

* edit a piece of writing;

* scan their edited piece independently onto an interactive whiteboard; and

* present work and explain the editing process.

DURATION

Three to four class periods.

PRIOR KNOWLEDGE REQUIRED

Students should have an understanding of

- the Writer's Workshop procedure (for more about this procedure, see *Launching the Writing Workshop* by Lucy Calkins and Leah Mermelstein),
- editors' jobs,
- how to edit,
- the need for all authors to have their writing edited, and
- how to use the interactive whiteboard and scanner.

VOCABULARY

Words to be introduced through this lesson:

exclamation mark
interactive whiteboard
"Look In"
punctuation
scanner
technology

Background

In the spring of 2005, Joan Vaughan, first-grade teacher at Waverly School, Eastchester, New York; John Blaser, technology integration specialist, Eastchester UFSD, Eastchester, New York; Carol Fisher, principal at Waverly School; and Mike Griffith, videoconferencing consultant and director of Global-Leap, partnered to set up a series of videoconferences between three Westchester (New York) County schools and three schools from the United Kingdom. Each U.S. principal selected first-grade teachers, and each U.K. head teacher selected second-year (U.S. first-grade equivalent) teachers to participate in the videoconferences. The primary aim of the project was to connect teachers from these schools to share their writing practices with each other and to converse about best practices in literacy.

Four videoconference sessions were held during the 2005–2006 school year. These sessions explored the similarities and differences in the writing process and how each teacher teaches writing to students. They also explored how we each integrate technology into our lessons. At our videoconferences the teachers had the opportunity to question, explore, and better understand each other's local and national standards as well as the way writing is actually taught. In conjunction with the videoconferences, a Blackboard site was created so that teachers could exchange ideas and thoughts about writing and view student work.

Prior to each videoconference, one class from the U.S. and one class from the U.K. each recorded a lesson being taught in their class and sent DVD copies to all participants so that we were all able to watch a teacher actually teaching her class how to write. Also, student work was posted on the Blackboard site.

The first videoconference included faculty member introductions and a description of the writing workshop model. Each teacher from the United States presented pieces of student writing that represented emerging, average, and proficient writers. During this videoconference we decided to continue this exchange for the 2005–2006 school year. It was further decided that we would send our New York State English Language Arts standards (http://usny.nysed.gov/teachers/nyslearningstandards.html) as well as Lucy Calkin's writing curriculum map (provided in her book *Launching the Writing Workshop*), which the Westchester County teachers follow. The teachers from the United Kingdom agreed to send us the National Literacy Strategy (www.standards.dcsf.gov.uk/nationalstrategies/) they are required to follow.

Prior to our March videoconference we adopted the model of a "Look-In," which we define as a live lesson being viewed at a remote-site classroom via videoconference. Following the model, Joan Vaughan taught a lesson on editing using a scanner and an interactive whiteboard. Teachers from St. Andrew's School in the United Kingdom watched the lesson via videoconference. At the conclusion of the lesson, the U.K. teachers were able to ask the first-grade Waverly students questions about using this technology to learn the lesson. At our videoconference a week later, all the teachers were able to discuss Joan's lesson. It was decided that each American school would partner with a U.K. school and do more of these "Look-Ins" during the 2006–2007 school year. We also decided to have the students begin to dialogue via videoconference and pen pal letters.

The collaboration among the American teachers (who never would have met otherwise) and with their counterparts in the United Kingdom has spurred a partnership of sharing and exchanging the best practices in literacy. It was a wonderful opportunity to learn that all teachers face the same challenges and rewards no matter their locations. It has enabled the teachers to receive more support in their teaching by means of the ongoing dialogue that can occur on the Blackboard site until we meet again via videoconference.

Pre-Conference Activities

Activity 1 • Editor's Rubric

Instructional Objective

After this activity students are able to create an editor's rubric in a whole-group setting. They are able to verbally state that editors need to look for capitalization, punctuation, and misspellings. They are able to edit a story displayed on the interactive whiteboard as well as one of their own pieces of writing.

Materials

- Interactive whiteboard or projector
- Paper, pencils

Procedure

1. **Mini Lesson.** Ask students to suggest things that editors do and chart their responses on the interactive whiteboard. Save this editor's rubric so that it can be referred to when needed. Discuss the need for all authors to have their pieces of writing edited. Students may make statements such as the following:

   - Editors need to check that all sentences begin with a capital letter.
   - Editors need to check that all special names, places, and things begin with a capital letter.
   - Editors need to check whether the writer uses periods, question marks, and exclamation marks in the right places.

   Reread the editor's rubric to the class, then present a teacher-created story on the interactive whiteboard. This story should have many punctuation and capitalization errors. Have the students come to the whiteboard and edit the story.

2. **Writing Conference.** Ask students to edit a piece of their own previously created writing (students maintain a "writing folder" that contains a collection of their writings). Meet with all students individually. Guide them to use the editor's rubric to help them with their editing and coach them where needed. These conferences may take place over a period of several days.

3. **Share Time.** Have the students read their written work aloud to the class and explain how they edited their work.

Evaluation

Evaluate students on their ability to edit (using capitals, correcting misspellings, and correcting punctuation) by conducting writing conferences and keeping records on these conferences.

Activity 2 • Adding Technology

Instructional Objective

This activity teaches students to easily integrate technology into the editing process. They learn to independently use a scanner and the interactive whiteboard.

Materials

- Interactive whiteboard
- Scanner
- Paper, pencils

Procedure

1. **Mini Lesson.** Gather students for instruction. Review the Mini-Lesson discussion from Activity 1, regarding the need for all authors to have their written pieces edited. Emphasize how we, as authors, need be good editors, too. Encourage students, "Wouldn't it be helpful if we could see our own writing on the interactive whiteboard? We could display it on the whiteboard to use during a mini lesson or view a student's work during share time." Using a piece of writing from a student's writing folder, demonstrate how to scan material onto the interactive whiteboard. Then, edit the student's work using responses from the group.

2. **Writing Conference.** Have the students return to their seats and continue editing pieces of their own writing. Meet with all students individually and help them with their editing. Have pairs of students meet with the technology integration specialist, who will model how to use the scanner, then observe and coach student scanner use.

3. **Share Time.** During the share time, have each pair of students demonstrate how to scan their writing pieces and display them on the interactive whiteboard.

Evaluation

Observe the students working together as a team to scan their writing pieces onto the interactive whiteboard. They should be able to explain to the class how to use the scanner and display their work on the interactive whiteboard.

Preparation for Videoconference

- Locate the United Kingdom on a globe with help from the class.
- Define "videoconference."
- Explain the reason for the "Look In."
- State behavioral expectations.
- Model and practice voice projection.

Videoconference

Topic: *Integration of technology in an editing lesson.*

Participants: *Teachers from St. Andrew's School, United Kingdom; First-grade class, Joan Vaughan (teacher), Waverly School, Eastchester, New York.*
Note: The remote classroom in the United Kingdom is able to see the data on Waverly School interactive whiteboard via the videoconference.

Introduction

Review the editor's rubric with the class. Together with the students, edit a student's scanned piece of writing on the interactive whiteboard. Circle misspellings, insert correct punctuation, and cross out letters that need to be capitalized and replace them with an uppercase letter. Move the misspelled words to a separate page in SMART Notebook (for users of SMART Boards) on the interactive whiteboard. In SMART Notebook separate the words into syllables and replace incorrect syllables with the correct spelling. This will provide a word-study lesson within the lesson.

Note: During the introduction and the student-activity part of the videoconference, the monitor showing the U.K. site should be turned off so as not to distract the students.

Activity and/or Presentation

Choose four students to participate in writing conferences during the videoconference. Write the names of these students on a chart visible to the U.K. teachers. Instruct the other students to go to their desks and begin editing a piece of their own writing from their writing folder.

During the writing conference time, coach the students and encourage them to refer to the rubrics when needed. After each conference, have the students scan their edited piece of writing onto the interactive whiteboard. The editor's rubrics should remain displayed on the interactive whiteboard until students begin scanning. During their share time have students present their pieces and show how they edited their work.

Question/Answer or Discussion

At the conclusion of the lesson, turn on the monitor that shows the U.K. site and instruct students to face the monitor. The students should be able to see the teachers from St. Andrew's School. Using dual video, the teachers at St. Andrew's School should be able to see scanned student work as well as the individual students. Students should greet the teachers by saying good morning and waving. They may be called on to answer any questions the teachers ask. Introduce the students who have scanned their writing and allow the "visiting" teachers to ask them questions.

Post-Conference Activities

Follow-up Activities

- Conduct a similar lesson with the students in the United Kingdom, having them become the writers and editors.

- Teachers at both sites can continue to discuss and study literacy standards, curriculum, differences and similarities in teaching practices, writer's workshops, and effective use of the interactive whiteboard during everyday lessons.

- Teachers can continue to conduct "Look Ins" in order to view lessons live in each other's classrooms.

- Expand learning opportunities by establishing partnerships among students via videoconference. Students can become pen pals. Once students become comfortable with far-site teachers, some team teaching may be done.

Mathematics

100th Day of School

LINDA MCDONALD
Katy Independent School District, Katy, Texas
Used with permission of Katy ISD, Katy, Texas.

TYPE OF LESSON:	*Collaborative Project*
GRADE LEVEL:	*PK–2*

The Evolution of Video Applications in Distance Education

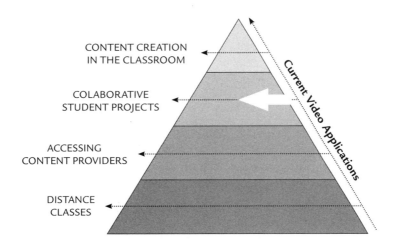

CORRELATION TO STANDARDS

Principles and Standards for School Mathematics

Numbers and Operations

NM-NUM.PK-2.1: Understand numbers, ways of representing numbers, relation-ships among numbers, and number systems. Expectations for Grades PK–2:

- count with understanding and recognize "how many" in sets of objects;

- use multiple models to develop initial understandings of place value and the base-ten number system;

- develop understanding of the relative position and magnitude of whole numbers and of ordinal and cardinal numbers and their connections

Algebra

NM-ALG.PK-2.1: Understand patterns, relations, and functions. Expectations for Grades PK–2:

- analyze how both repeating and growing patterns are generated

Reprinted with permission. © 2000 by the National Council of Teachers of Mathematics.

Standards for the English Language Arts

NL-ENG.K-12.4 Communication Skills

Students adjust their use of spoken, written, and visual language (e.g., conven-tions, style, vocabulary) to communicate effectively with a variety of audiences and for different purposes.

Reprinted with permission. © 1996 by the International Reading Association and the National Council of Teachers of English. Available at www.ncte.org/standards/.

UNIT GOAL

To celebrate the 100th day of school by counting and sharing activities.

LESSON OBJECTIVES

After completing this lesson, students will be able to

- count to 100 by 1s, 2s, 5s, and 10s;

- describe a pattern and determine what comes next; and

- describe an activity or project to an interactive audience.

DURATION

Multiple 30-minute sessions on the 100th day of school (varies organization to organization).

PRIOR KNOWLEDGE REQUIRED

Students should have an understanding of

- 100s charts,
- color patterns, and
- a 100th Day activity selected by teacher (see Activity 2).

Pre-Conference Activities

Activity 1 • Daily Calendar Math

Instructional Objective

Students participate in routine practice of number concept skills and other basic concepts as determined by local curriculum guides.

Materials

Adopted calendar math program (varies based on local curriculum adoption)

See Scholastic's Calendar Math Activities page (http://teacher.scholastic.com/fieldtrp/k2/calendar.htm) for additional information and resources. Look for examples of how to describe a number to build students' number concepts.

Additional suggested calendar activities and resources can be found on Mrs. Nelson's Class page (www.mrsnelsonsclass.com/teacherresources/teachingmath/dailycalendar.aspx).

Procedure

See adopted calendar math program for suggested procedures. Mrs. Meacham's Classroom Snapshots site (www.jmeacham.com/calendar/calendar.htm) gives a wonderful step-by-step process if needed.

Evaluation

Teacher evaluates specific skills as needed.

Activity 2 • Preparing for 100th Day

Instructional Objective

Students learn to count to 100 in a variety of ways.

Materials

See the following websites for specific ideas and assignments:

- A to Z Teacher Stuff: 100th Day links:
  www.atozteacherstuff.com/Themes/100th_Day/

- Enchanted Learning—100th Day theme
  www.enchantedlearning.com/themes/hundred.shtml

- Math Forum—100th Day of School
  http://mathforum.org/t2t/faq/faq.100.html

- Scholastic Themes & Teaching Ideas—100th Day of School
  www2.scholastic.com/browse/collection.jsp?id=144

- Southern Indiana Education Center's 100th Day of School Celebration:
  www.siec.k12.in.us/~west/proj/100th/act.htm

Procedure

The 100th Day of School is a celebration that teachers prepare students for through daily calendar math activities (see Activity 1). The final preparation includes a special activity that will be used, or will take place, on the celebration day. Teachers usually prepare several centers that are related to this celebration. Students should be able to describe the product or activity to others during the videoconference session.

Evaluation

Teacher observation of student products.

Preparation for Videoconference

- Provide overview of behavior expectations during videoconference.
- Create and display sign noting school name and location.
- Develop student questions (see Pre-Conference Activity 2).

Videoconference

Topic: *100th day of school.*

Participants: *Facilitator, two-to-four intradistrict sites.*

Overview

This project requires a facilitator to direct all activity and discussion among the sites. Prior to the videoconference the facilitator prepares four 100s charts. These can be used for multiple sessions. See www.enchantedlearning.com/math/hundred/100.shtml if a sample is needed. The charts are color coded as follows:

- Chart 1: uncolored
- Chart 2: color coded to assist students in counting by 2s (2, 4, 6...)
- Chart 3: color coded to assist students in counting by 5s (5, 10, 15...)
- Chart 4: color coded to assist students in counting by 10s (10, 20,30...)

This facilitator begins the videoconference with the Introduction activities, displaying materials on a document camera. The facilitator calls on participating sites to invite their sharing activity. If time allows, the facilitator concludes with an appropriate grade-level activity and the session closing finale (a song).

Introduction

1. Roll Call

   a. Color in one square for each class on 100s chart to keep a running tally of the project participants. The district goal is to connect 100 classes on the 100th day of school. Students make a prediction about whether or not this goal will be met. Send a copy of the completed chart to participating classes for review as appropriate.

   b. On the 100s chart, use three colors to color in squares to create an ABC color pattern (e.g., color square 1 yellow, square 2 blue, square 3 green, and square 4 yellow again). Solicit responses from students with questions such as: "What color comes next in this pattern?" and "How can this pattern be described?"

2. Use the color-coded 100s charts, displayed on the document camera, to assist students in counting to 100. All classes count along while the facilitator points to appropriate numbers. All classes should mute their microphones so the time delay does not create an echo-type feedback.

   a. Have the class count to 100 by 1s (use Chart 1).

   b. Have the class count to 100 by 2s (use Chart 2).

   c. Have the class count to 100 by 5s (use Chart 3).

   d. Have the class count to 100 by 10s (use Chart 4).

   e. If time allows, ask each class for other ways to count to 100 (e.g., by 3s or 4s).

Facilitator may choose whether or not to engage students in that counting sequence based on time allotment and grade-level appropriateness.

Activity and/or Presentation

Each class shares an activity (see Pre-Conference Activity 2). This should be something you are already doing in your classroom: a song, a poem, a fashion show of something made by the students, for example. The simpler, the better. The goal is to get students engaged; so they should do the talking if possible. If time allows include the following grade-appropriate activity and the sesson closing finale.

PK–K students: 100 Movements

Students should perform 10 repetitions of each exercise:

- touch toes
- clap hands
- jump on both feet
- shrug shoulders
- do jumping jacks
- wiggle all over
- hop on one foot
- touch shoulders
- snap fingers
- blink

Grade 1 students: Comparing Numbers

Each class brings a deck of playing cards. Remove all face cards and 10s. In this activity an ace equals 1.

Each site flips two cards face up on the document camera. If a document camera is not available, the cards can be held up for the main camera to zoom in on. At each site students read the two cards, left to right, as a single two-digit number, e.g., a five of hearts and a two of spades would be read as the number 52. After all sites have read their numbers, review the responses provided by each site. Ask students from one site to determine the highest number and students from a different site to determine the lowest number. Prompt students to explain, "How do you know that is the highest number?" This activity can be repeated if time allows.

Grade 2 students: Addition

Each class brings a deck of playing cards. Remove all face cards and 10s. In this activity an ace equals 1.

Flip two cards on the document camera and explain to students how to read the two cards as a two-digit number. For example, a five of hearts and a two of spades would be read as the number 52.

Have each site flip two cards on their document camera. If a document camera is not available, the teacher or a student can hold up the cards and use the main camera to zoom in. Ask each site to add your two-digit number to their two-digit number. Students should work in small groups within their local site. Allow one minute for students to calculate responses. Rotate among sites and prompt students to explain their solutions, showing their work on the document camera. Call on one site to determine the highest sum and another site to determine the lowest sum. If time allows, have each site create and share a word problem that correlates to the two-digit problem just solved.

Session Closing: Finale

Have students sing the following song to the tune of "Ta-ra-ra Boom-de-ay":

> It's the 100th day.
> So shout hip-hip hooray!
> We'll count and eat and play,
> On the 100th day!
>
> See all we've collected.
> 100s on display.
> Join in the fun and say,
> Hooray for the 100th Day!

Post-Conference Activities

Follow-up Activity • Celebration of 100th Day

Activity selection is based on teacher preference. Activities could include:

a. A day of math centers/stations. See pre-conference Activity 2 for resources that include ideas for crafts and measurement activities. Students rotate between centers/stations. Parent volunteers can be used to help with management.

b. A parade through the school. Students wear t-shirts, hats, and jewelry that each represent 100. Or students dress up like they are 100 years old.

c. In art, students create a 100s collage/poster.

d. In music, students sing 100th Day songs.

e. In P.E., students do 100 exercises.

f. A visit by Zero the Hero—see two classroom examples:

- www.owensborocatholic.org/schools/K-3/photo_album/Zero_The_Hero

- http://mrskilburnkiddos.wordpress.com/math/numbers-and-counting/zero-the-hero/

Awesome Insects: Scram, Squash, or Study?

LISA PRIDE, Distance Learning Instructor
    Southeast Kansas Education Service Center, Greenbush, Girard, Kansas

TYPE OF LESSON:	*Distance Class*
GRADE LEVEL:	3–4

The Evolution of Video Applications in Distance Education

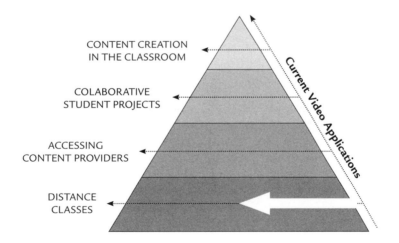

CORRELATION TO STANDARDS

National Science Education Standards

NS.K-4.1 Science as Inquiry

As a result of activities in Grades K–4, all students should develop:

- Abilities necessary to do scientific inquiry

- Understanding about scientific inquiry

NS.K-4.3 Life Science

As a result of activities in Grades K–4, all students should develop understanding of:

- The characteristics of organisms

    - Organisms have basic needs.

    - Each plant or animal has different structures that serve different functions in growth, survival, and reproduction.

    - The behavior of individual organisms is influenced by internal cues (such as hunger) and by external cues (such as a change in the environment).

- Life cycles of organisms

    - Plants and animals have life cycles that include being born, developing into adults, reproducing, and eventually dying.

    - Many characteristics of an organism are inherited from the parents of the organism, but other characteristics result from an individual's interactions with the environment.

- Organisms and their environments

    - All animals depend on plants.

    - An organism's patterns of behavior are related to the nature of that organism's environment, including the kinds and numbers of other organisms present, the availability of food and resources, and the physical characteristics of the environment.

Reprinted with permission. © 1995 by the National Academy of Sciences, Courtesy of the National Academies Press, Washington, D.C.

UNIT GOAL

To be able to develop an understanding of characteristics, life cycles, and survival of insects.

LESSON OBJECTIVES

After completing this lesson, students will be able to

- identify body parts of an insect, including head, thorax, abdomen, antennae, and wings;

- construct a life-cycle wheel, including the four stages of the butterfly life cycle;

- explain how adaptations (physical and behavioral) help insects survive in their environments; and

- apply newly acquired information to complete the insect-adaptation project.

DURATION

Three class sessions of 45–60 minutes each.

VOCABULARY

Words to be introduced through this lesson:

abdomen
adaptation
adult
antennae
compound eyes
egg
exoskeleton
forewings
habitat
head
hindwings
larva
metamorphosis
proboscis
pupa
scales
simple eyes
thorax

Pre-Conference Activities

Preparation for Videoconference

- Explain how the videoconferencing equipment works, behavior expectations, and procedures for asking and responding to questions.
- Make tent-style student nametags with large print.
- E-mail student list to the distance instructor.
- Gather any supplies and materials necessary for completing the lesson plan.
- Review vocabulary words and meanings.
- Make sure equipment is turned on and ready prior to program.

Videoconference—Day One

Topic: *Insect characteristics*

Content Provider: *Distance instructor*

Materials

- "Awesome Insects" digital presentation
- Insect diagram
- Madagascar hissing roaches in individual containers (roaches available from www.nyworms.com/roaches.htm)
- Exploring Insects worksheet
- Hand lenses
- Rulers

Introduction

Ask students, "How many of you watch the television show *Fear Factor*? If you watch the show you have probably seen these creatures before." Show hissing roaches on the document camera. "Does anyone know what these are?" Accept answers until a student identifies they are Madagascar hissing roaches, a type of insect.

Activities and/or Presentation

Use the Awesome Insects digital presentation to guide lesson.

Ask the following questions to assess prior knowledge: "How do we know an insect is an insect? What are their characteristics?" Make a list of the characteristics students already know.

Use the insect diagram to discuss characteristics and body parts of an insect and how they use particular body parts for survival in their environment. Include the following: exoskeleton, head, thorax, abdomen, six legs, antennae, wings, and eyes.

Have the facilitator at each site instruct students on the proper way to safely handle the roaches. Direct the facilitator to distribute the live Madagascar hissing roaches and have students complete the Exploring Insects worksheet in cooperative groups of three to four students.

Discuss answers to the Exploring Insects worksheet using a presentation tool (such as PowerPoint) to summarize and document answers to student questions.

Question/Answer or Discussion

During this time students can ask questions about insects in general or specific questions about the Madagascar hissing roaches. This session will last 5–10 minutes.

Evaluation

Use the Exploring Insects worksheet to evaluate student participation.

Videoconference—Day Two

Topic: *Life cycles and characteristics of butterflies.*

Teacher Materials

- Life-cycles presentation
- Butterfly display
- Butterfly diagram
- Life-cycle wheel sample

Student Materials

- 9-inch paper plate
- Three to five small shell pasta (representing eggs)
- 3-inch brown or green pipe cleaner (representing larva)
- One large macaroni noodle (representing pupa)
- One bow-tie noodle (representing adult butterfly)
- Crayons or markers

Introduction

Present the butterfly display that shows many brightly colored butterflies and ask, "Where do butterflies come from?" Accept all answers and discuss anything students remember from previous learning about life cycles.

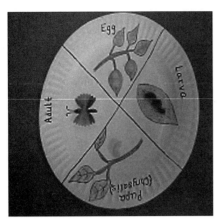

Life-cycle wheel

Activities and/or Presentation

Use the life-cycles presentation to introduce all stages of the life cycle, discussing each stage in great detail.

Use the butterfly diagram to discuss all characteristics and body parts of an adult butterfly. Make sure to include the following: head, thorax, abdomen, six legs, forewings, hind wings, antennae, compound eyes, scales, and proboscis.

Check for understanding by reviewing life cycles using review questions.

Using the student materials, have students create a life-cycle wheel that includes all four stages of the butterfly life cycle (see figure). Allow question and answer time while students are making their life-cycle wheels.

When they finish, have students share their completed life-cycle wheels on the document camera.

Evaluation

Grade life-cycle wheel activity for accuracy.

Videoconference—Day Three

Topic: *Insect adaptation*

Teacher Materials

- Animal pictures (elephant, giraffe, porcupine, etc.)
- Live animals (any live animal that has a physical adaptation)
- Digital camera
- Equipment for creating a podcast

Experiment Materials

- Clear disposable cups (9 oz.)
- Paper towels
- Rubber bands
- Styrofoam bowls
- Water bottles—half full (16 or 20 oz.)
- Paper plates
- Packing peanuts (broken into little pieces)

- Clothespins
- Sponges (cut into 1-inch squares)
- Straws
- Coffee stir straws (one end cut to a sharp point)

Student Materials
- Insect Adaptation worksheet
- Insect Habitat worksheet
- Madagascar hissing roaches
- Potato (one per student)
- Tempera paint
- Miscellaneous art supplies

Experiment Stations
Set up experiment materials in stations before the lesson begins.

Station 1   Water bottle, empty cup, tool bag*

Station 2   Cup that is full of water, covered with a paper towel and secured with a rubber band; empty cup; tool bag*

Station 3   Styrofoam bowl that is half full of water, empty bowl, tool bag*

Station 4   Paper plate with packing peanuts on it, empty plate, tool bag*

Tool bag contains: 1 clothespin, 1 straw, 1 coffee stir straw, 1 clothespin with sponge attached.

Introduction
Tell your students, "Every animal has special features that help it survive in its habitat. They can be physical features or behavioral features. Let's look at pictures of animals with some of these features." Show an elephant picture and ask, "Why do elephants have a long trunk and tusks?" Show a picture of a giraffe and ask, "Why do giraffes have long necks?" Introduce the vocabulary word *adaptation* and give the definition.

Activities or Presentation
Following the introduction, brainstorm with students about animals with adaptations. Make a list of animals, including their adaptation, and determine if their adaptation is physical or behavioral. Discuss how these adaptations help the animals survive in their habitats.

Ask the facilitators in the classroom to pass out the Madagascar hissing roaches and ask students to identify physical and behavioral adaptations of this insect. Point out the "chewing" mouth of the roach and mention that it is designed to eat decaying plants and animals on the forest floor. Ask, "Why is it important that insects have different kinds of mouths?" Emphasize that if all animals had the same mouth they would all have to eat the same things, which would make food supplies scarce.

Have students work in cooperative groups and rotate through each station, trying to determine which tool (insect mouth) from the tool bag works best for gathering the "food" at each station and transferring it to the empty container. After completion of the experiment discuss which tool worked best for each container.

Station 1. The straw will work best because it is long enough to reach the water in the bottle. The straw represents the mouth of a butterfly.

Station 2. The coffee stir straw will work best because it can poke through the paper towel to reach the water below. The coffee stir straw represents the mouth of a mosquito.

Station 3. The clothespin with sponge will work best because it gathered a large amount of water from the bowl. This tool represents insects that have a lapping mouth.

Station 4. The clothespin will work best for biting and chewing the food. The clothespin represents chewing mouths like that of the hissing roaches.

Insect adaptation

Explain the insect adaptation project. Have students work in cooperative groups to research an assigned habitat (desert, tropical rainforest, etc.) to determine what special adaptations an insect would need to survive there. Give each group an Insect Habitat worksheet to guide their research. After researching, the groups will design and build a new insect to live in that habitat and complete the Insect Adaptation worksheet about their creature. The groups can then take a picture of their new insect and create an audio or video podcast to publish on their school website and send to the distance-learning instructor.

Evaluation

The insect adaptation project will be assessed based on a rubric system. The rubric should include criteria such as

- adaptations match to habitat conditions,
- completeness of research,
- completion of insect model,
- photo of insect created,
- quality of podcast, and
- team effort.

AWESOME INSECTS: SCRAM, SQUASH, OR STUDY?

Exploring Insects

Remove your roach from the container. Identify the head, thorax, and abdomen.

Is your roach a male or female? How do you know?

Estimate the length of your roach. _____

How do you think your roach defends itself?

Place your roach on your desk or table. What does it do? Describe its behavior.

Write down one question you have about this insect.

AWESOME INSECTS: SCRAM, SQUASH, OR STUDY?

Insect Habitat

Your group's habitat is: _____

Yearly rainfall: _____

Average daily temperature: _____

What is the ground covering? Grass? Sand? Rocks? and so forth.

Are there natural water sources in this region? If so, what is available? Streams, lakes, rivers, oceans?

What kinds of plants grow here?

What animals live here?

AWESOME INSECTS: SCRAM, SQUASH, OR STUDY?

Insect Adaptation

Answer the following questions and describe any adaptations that help the insect complete these activities in order to survive in its habitat.

What is the name of your insect?

What does it eat?

How will it obtain food and water?

How will it keep warm/cool?

Where will it take shelter?

How will it protect/defend itself from predators?

If your insect didn't have these adaptations, what problems might it face?

Impacting Local History

DIANE NYE, Media Specialist
  E. P. Clarke Elementary School, St. Joseph, Michigan

LINDA MCCONVILLE, Fourth-Grade Teacher
  E.P. Clarke Elementary School, St. Joseph Michigan

TYPE OF LESSON:	*Collaborative Project*
GRADE LEVEL:	*4–6*

The Evolution of Video Applications in Distance Education

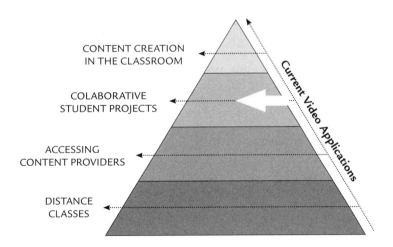

CORRELATION TO STANDARDS

National Standards for History

NSS-USH.K-4.2 The History of Students' Own State or Region

- The student understands the people, events, problems, and ideas that were significant in creating the history of their state

NSS-USH.K-4.4 The history of peoples of many cultures around the world

- The student understands selected attributes and historical developments of societies in Africa, the Americas, Asia, and Europe

Reprinted with permission. © 1996 National Center for History in the Schools, UCLA, http://nchs.ucla.edu

UNIT GOAL

Using the Big6 lesson plan model, students learn about historical individuals who have made an impact on the local community.

LESSON OBJECTIVES

After completing this lesson, students will be able to

- identify and appreciate the accomplishments and philanthropy of historical individuals from our local community,

- use and organize a problem-solving approach to research, and

- apply the protocol for interacting during a videoconference.

DURATION

Two to three class periods.

PRIOR KNOWLEDGE REQUIRED

Students should have an understanding that

- parks and schools are often named after prominent individuals,

- information exists in multiple formats and places, and

- students from other schools have many of the same interests.

VOCABULARY

Words to be introduced through this lesson:

ancestors
brainstorming
civic leader
graphic organizer
manufacturer
philanthropy
primary documents
prominent
prosperous
public affairs
spouse
tribute
webbing

Pre-Conference Activities

Activity 1 • Calling All Colors

Community Workshop for Elementary Students (off-site)

Calling All Colors (www.coastal.edu/cec/calling.html) is an innovative program for elementary school–aged students that unites students from various ethnic backgrounds who otherwise might not have the opportunity to interact.

Instructional Objective

The instructional objective is to heighten awareness and sensitivity to cultural diversity, enhance self-esteem, and reduce anxiety about interacting with people of different racial or ethnic backgrounds.

Procedure

Students travel to a local Boys and Girls Club to participate in the Calling All Colors program. In this program, trained facilitators unite fourth-graders from differing schools to interact through games, exercise, small group activities, and role-playing in a workshop format.

Evaluation

Students journal about their reactions to the Calling All Colors experience.

Activity 2 • Schools and Parks

Instructional Objective

To determine previous knowledge about names that students see on schools and parks in the local community.

Materials

Multiple-choice pre-test on historical community individuals whom students will later research

Procedure

Give pre-test.

Evaluation

Record results to compare with post-test.

Preparation for Videoconference

Students and parents receive a letter explaining the videoconference procedure and dates and times of the conference. See the following sample letter:

Dear students:

This school year you'll be doing a videoconferencing project with another fourth-grade class just like yours.

This will be unlike anything you've ever done. This isn't like TV—it is not the same quality and you won't be just watching the big screen. You get to "talk back" to the class you'll see on the screen, and the other sites involved in the connection can see you during the videoconference.

You may also see your class on the screen. An extra monitor or picture-in-picture lets you observe what the other site is seeing. When you first see yourself on camera, it's tempting to wave and make faces. But don't forget that the other class is watching you!

Videoconferencing uses compression to code the audio (talking) and video (picture), send it over six digital phone lines, and then decode it on the other side. This happens simultaneously on both ends. You may notice a slight delay when you talk to each other. This is normal. Just wait a little longer for an answer.

The things to remember during the videoconference are:

- Keep your curiosity.
- Don't be afraid to ask questions about what you learn.
- Speak up when you talk.
- Enjoy your project!

Sample student letter

Videoconference

Topic: *Introducing the Big6 research model.*

Participants: *Our school and our partner school connecting over IP.*

Introduction

The videoconference begins with an interactive discussion about personal and community names and how names of landmarks are derived. Questions from Beth Goodman's book *What's Your Name?* are used to start the discussion.

Activity and/or Presentation

Have students complete the following activities. These activities follow the six steps of the information processing model. These activities may take from four to six videoconference sessions.

1. **Task Definition.** What do I need to do?
   Activity: Select names to study and list questions to focus the research.

2. **Information-Seeking Strategies.** What resources can I use?
   Activity: Brainstorm different types of information sources.

3. **Location and Access.** Where can I find these sources?
   Activity: Develop a list of community and school research resources.

4. **Use of Information.** What information do I need?
   Activity: Note-taking practice on a graphic organizer using a biography about Sojourner Truth.

5. **Synthesis.** How can I put my information together?
   Activity: Break into small groups at each site to work on gathering information to share with whole group.

6. **Evaluation.** How will I know I did a good job?
   Activity: Presentation of final research on the designated name.

Post-Conference Activities

Follow-up Activity: Publishing Our Research and Post-Test

Instructional Objectives

- Create a final project of both classes' research that can be shared with the school and community.

- Administer post-test to determine growth in understanding of the importance of the person behind the name.

Materials

Written reports and photos relating to each of the historical names.

Evaluation

Student completes the following test and survey:

- Readministered multiple-choice test from Pre-Conference Activity 2

- Survey assessing mastery of Big6 information-processing skills

Chapter 3

Middle School Lessons

Reading and Language Arts
Author Visit with Patricia McKissack

Mathematics
Math Marvels

Science
Mammals, Mammoths, Manatees!

Social Studies
Genocide Study

Author Visit
with Patricia McKissack

MARTHA BOGART
   Virtual Learning Center, Cooperating School Districts
   of Greater St. Louis, St. Louis, Missouri

TYPE OF LESSON:	*Content Expert*
GRADE LEVEL:	*5–6*

The Evolution of Video Applications in Distance Education

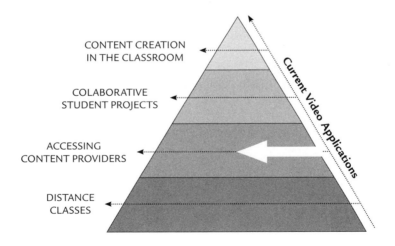

CORRELATION TO STANDARDS

Standards for the English Language Arts

NL-ENG.K-12.1 Reading for Perspective

Students read a wide range of print and non print texts to build an understanding of texts, of themselves, and of the cultures of the United States and the world; to acquire new information; to respond to the needs and demands of society and the workplace; and for personal fulfillment. Among these texts are fiction and nonfiction, classic and contemporary works

NL-ENG.K-12.3 Evaluation Strategies

Students apply a wide range of strategies to comprehend, interpret, evaluate, and appreciate texts. They draw on their prior experience, their interactions with other readers and writers, their knowledge of word meaning and of other texts, their word identification strategies, and their understanding of textual features (e.g., sound-letter correspondence, sentence structure, context, graphics).

NL-ENG.K-12.4 Communication Skills

Students adjust their use of spoken, written, and visual language (e.g., conventions, style, vocabulary) to communicate effectively with a variety of audiences and for different purposes.

NL-ENG.K-12.5 Communication Strategies

Students employ a wide range of strategies as they write and use different writing process elements appropriately to communicate with different audiences for a variety of purposes.

Reprinted with permission. © 1996 by the International Reading Association and the National Council of Teachers of English. Available at www.ncte.org/standards/.

UNIT GOALS

- Students will understand how to research different winter holidays around the world and use this research to create fictional stories about them.

- Students will understand the basic elements of a story.

- Essential questions: How and why are holidays celebrated? Why do people tell stories?

LESSON OBJECTIVES

After completing this lesson, students will be able to

- research winter holidays celebrated around the world,

- create a fictional story about one of the winter holidays celebrated around the world,

- critique stories in a peer review manner, and

- ask pertinent questions of an author about the writing process.

DURATION

Flexible; 2–3 weeks.

PRIOR KNOWLEDGE REQUIRED

Students should have an understanding of

- Patricia McKissack's biography, and
- *Can You Imagine?* by Patricia McKissack.

VOCABULARY

Words to be introduced through this lesson:

action
character
idea
setting

Pre-Conference Activities

Activity 1 • Holiday Story

Instructional Objective

To provide a starting point and an example of a holiday story written by the author who will participate in the videoconference.

Materials

Christmas in the Big House, Christmas in the Quarters, by Patricia McKissack

Procedure

1. Read, with the class, *Christmas in the Big House, Christmas in the Quarters,* by Patricia McKissack, showing the illustrations in the book.

2. Elicit questions and comments about the book by using higher-order questioning strategies. Generate a list of questions. Start the list with a few questions, including:

   • What do each of the celebrations in the book have in common?

   • Why are they different?

   • How do the pictures contribute to the story?

   • How do you celebrate special holidays in your family?

Evaluation

Give students a teacher-designed comprehension quiz on the book.

Activity 2 • Author Questions

Instructional Objective

To prepare students for the videoconference with McKissack by having them think about how holidays are celebrated and what questions they would like to ask her.

Materials

How I Celebrate worksheet

Procedure

1. Discuss the topic of winter holidays and the fact that many holidays are celebrated around the world at this time of year. Stress the idea that everyone does not participate in the same holidays and celebrations, and that this is okay. Explain that the class members will share some of the ways they celebrate the winter holidays and what makes it a special time for them.

2. Have students fill out the How I Celebrate worksheet. Here are some leading questions to ask:

   - Do you participate in a formal holiday celebration?

   - Do you take part in community activities?

   - Do you celebrate at home with friends or family?

   - Do you have special meals, exchange gifts, attend religious services?

   - Do you enjoy seeing relatives, getting presents, sleeping in, hanging out at the mall, skiing?

   - What are your earliest memories of this time of year and the celebrations surrounding it?

   - Do you remember where you went, what you did, and the relatives who said how much you've grown?

   - Do the memories feel special?

   - What does the holiday mean to you?

   - Is it about love, faith, hope, or peace?

   - Is it a time of community and sharing, or solitude and reflection?

   - Does it mean the same to others in your family?

Explain to the students that they are not required to provide any personal information that they are uncomfortable sharing with the rest of the class. See student samples (pp. 61–62).

3. Discuss students' responses in class.

4. Have students come up with questions they want to ask McKissack during the videoconference. Select spokespersons to ask these questions. Have the questions written out so that time will not be wasted during the videoconference.

5. Practice the protocol of the videoconference with the students. You may want to go to the distance-learning room and do this. If this is not practical, set up a "pretend" microphone and have students come to the front of the room and practice asking their questions in a clear voice, stating their name and school first.

Evaluation

Check worksheet and review questions students have written for McKissack.

Preparation for Videoconference

The following tasks are completed to prepare for the videoconference:

- Review behavioral expectations for the videoconference. Students sign a behavior contract.

- Create and display a tent sign noting school name and location.

- Develop and write down student questions. Review the procedure for interaction with the class during the videoconference.

Videoconference: Day One

Topic: *How to write a story*

Content Provider: *author Patricia McKissack; Cooperating School Districts, St. Louis, MO*

Activity and/or Presentation

Patricia McKissack presents a talk on the writing process and how an author writes a story. She focuses on how she researched her book *Christmas in the Big House, Christmas in the Quarters* and how she incorporated her research into the book. She then asks the students to describe how they celebrate winter holidays at their house. Students use their How I Celebrate worksheets to respond. McKissack then introduces students to the WAVE method of starting a story (see WAVE Method handout) and has the students help her create one.

After the question and answer time, the author assigns the students to write an original story about one of the following winter holidays: Christmas, Hanukkah, Ramadan, New Year's Day, Kwanzaa, Winter Solstice, Chinese New Year. Students share these stories in a follow-up videoconference with McKissack and get feedback about their work from her. They are allowed to e-mail her with questions if they wish.

Question/Answer or Discussion

There is a 15-minute question and answer time for the students to ask their prepared questions about the writing process.

Post-Conference Activities

Follow-up Activity

Instructional Objective

Students create an original holiday story for critique by their peers and the author.

Materials

- Themes on Hanukkah
  www.emints.org/ethemes/resources/S00000249.shtml
- Themes on Kwanzaa
  www.emints.org/ethemes/resources/S00000250.shtml
- Themes on Christmas
  www.emints.org/ethemes/resources/S00000500.shtml
  www.emints.org/ethemes/resources/S00000501.shtml

- Themes on Ramadan
  www.teachersfirst.com/autoframe.htm?
  www.teachersfirst.com/ramadan.htm

- Themes on Winter Solstice
  www.emints.org/ethemes/resources/S00001376.shtml

- Themes on Chinese New Year
  www.emints.org/ethemes/resources/S00000612.shtml

- Themes on Literature: Story Elements
  www.emints.org/ethemes/resources/S00000236.shtml

- Themes on Writing Fiction
  www.emints.org/ethemes/resources/S00000243.shtml

- Handout 1—The WAVE Technique, Handout 2—Definitions of Terms in Writing, and Handout 3—Ways to Research

Procedure

1. Put students in groups of four.

2. Have each group select a winter holiday from the list provided. Each group member has a role to play in the group. Two people are the researchers.

3. Using the questions generated during class discussions, students use the materials (websites) provided to find out information about their holiday. Using the web resources provided, the other two group members research how to write fiction.

4. Each student should use a graphic organizer to collect and sort information and bring this back to the group to share. Students share their information with each other.

5. Provide a pre-writing graphic organizer to the students and encourage them to come up with a plan for writing their stories. They decide if they need to do more research and who will do what in their collaborative writing effort.

6. Circulate around the room to help each group and suggest certain tasks that the group needs to accomplish, such as brainstorming ideas for the story, drafting the story, and creating illustrations for the story.

7. Discuss with the class how the stories will be evaluated and have the students develop a scoring guide or peer review sheet.

8. Using the plans they created, students begin creating their stories. They should use word processing software for this and a paint program to create their illustrations.

9. Circulate around the room, helping students.

10. Students are allowed to contact the author, Patricia McKissack, through e-mail (teacher facilitated) to get feedback about their stories in progress and ask questions about how she wrote her story. The group member who did the research on the author directs this part of the process.

11. Students select short sections of their stories to read aloud to McKissack during the follow-up videoconference. (A document camera should be available to show student illustrations.) Students develop specific questions to ask her about their stories, which will help them to revise them. It is helpful to follow this model: 1) Praise: What do you like about my work? Be specific. 2) Question: What questions do you have about my work? Is anything confusing to you? If so, what? 3) Polish: What one thing could I do to improve my work?

Evaluation

Students monitor their progress through a series of revisions using peer review. Final drafts are evaluated on these criteria, which are included in a rubric that the students were given at the beginning of the writing process:

- Accurate facts about each holiday included in the story
- Story shows an understanding of the holiday depicted
- Story contains all elements of effective storytelling
- Illustrations match and enhance content
- Story grabs and holds the interest of the reader
- Minimal grammatical, syntactical, and spelling errors

Videoconference: Day Two

Topic: *Feedback on written work.*

Content Provider: *author Patricia McKissack; Cooperating School Districts, St. Louis, Missouri.*

Activity and/or Presentation

Patricia McKissack listens as students read their stories aloud and gives critical feedback so that the students can revise their work. In addition, if there are several classes connected
at the same time, students from remote locations can gave feedback to each other.

This lesson and all of the handouts mentioned can be found on the web at: www2.csd.org/newlinks/McKissack/index.htm

How I Celebrate

1. How do you celebrate the kolidays?

2. Do you participate in a formal holiday celebration?

3. Do you celebrate at home with friends or family?

4. Do you take part in community activities?

5. Do you have special meals, exchange gifts, attend church, synagogue, temple or mosque?

6. Do you enjoy seeing relatives, getting presents, sleeping in, hanging out at the mall, skiing?

7. What are your earliest memories of this time of year and the celebrations surrounding it?

8. Do you remember where you went, what you did, and the relatives who pinched your cheek?

9. Do the memories feel special? Why or why not?

10. What does the holiday mean to you? is it about love, faith, hope, or peace?

11. Is it a time of community and sharing, or solitude and reflection?

12. Does it mean the same to others in your family?

AUTHOR VISIT WITH PATRICIA MCKISSACK

The WAVE Technique

How to begin a story

1. Write a statement.

2. Support the statement with action.

3. Support the statement with dialogue.

4. Write a clincher.

Example

(1) Mary was tired. (2) She kicked off her boots and flopped in the chair by the fireplace. (3) "I always forget something and have to go shopping on Christmas Eve. Never again," Mary said, sighing. (4) Just then, she heard the laughter of children approaching her house.

AUTHOR VISIT WITH PATRICIA MCKISSACK

Definition of Terms in Writing

Character

This is WHO the story is about. What is the person's name and what is he or she like? What does this person look like? What is the person's personality? Is the person mean? Funny? Gentle? Sad? The way you describe a character in a book is not by telling, but by showing. For example, instead of saying "Mary was tall," you might say "Mary was taller than all of her friends in the third grade." The way you describe a character is through what the character says and what he or she does. This leads to ACTION.

Action

This is WHAT is happening in the story. What are the characters doing? What happens first? Next? Last? Remember to use transitions to show movement from one thing to another. These are words or phrases such as "then," "all at once," "suddenly," and so forth. This action has to take place somewhere, which leads to SETTING.

Setting

This is WHERE the story takes place and WHEN it takes place. What is the country? Town? What year is it? Month? Time of day? What type of building is it in? And so forth. Always be sure to let your reader know when time has passed. For example, "When morning came..."

Idea

This is why you wrote the story. This is the MEANING of the story. What is your point? What do you want your readers to understand from the story after they have read it? You don't want your reader to finish reading the story and then say "So what?" However, you do not want to tell your reader the point of your story directly. Never tell your reader what to think or what to feel. Instead, let the story itself bring out thoughts and feelings.

AUTHOR VISIT WITH PATRICIA MCKISSACK

Ways to Research

Interviews

- Telephone
- Letters
- E-mail
- Personal chats

Library

- Books
- Periodicals

Museums

Historical Societies

Historic Houses

Trips or Tours

Student Samples

Christmas in Missouri

BY CONSTANCE, CARLOTTA, AND STEPHON

Three inches of snow had settled on the cabin roof. Joy woke up Mama, and Peace woke up Papa.

"It's snowing! It's snowing!" screamed Merry. "Can we get the Christmas tree?" the children begged. The children put on their clothing and they went outside. They looked for a beautiful green pine tree. Then they cut down the tree and brought the tree in the house. The children took off their clothing and hung it on the hangers in their room.

Then Merry asked, "Peace, will you help Mama and me bake the fruit cake?"

"No."

Merry said, "But Mama and I need help. Please, Peace, will you help us?"

"Okay, I will."

Papa and Joy went to the dining room to make some ornaments for the tree. They had already gathered pinecones from the woods. Each of them decorated them with different color icing. They put them on the Christmas tree when they were done. Papa and Joy smelled something good in the kitchen. It smelled like Juicy Fruit gum. Papa and Joy knew it was the delicious fruit cake that Mama, Peace, and Merry had made.

"Mmm, Mmm good," said everyone at once. Papa said, "We all need some time alone to make our Christmas gifts."

The dining room was turned into a workshop. Papa made a rocking horse for Merry. Merry made a toy cart for Peace. Joy sewed a skirt for Mama. Mama made a stocking with all Joy's favorite cookies in it. Peace made a special box for Papa's tools. Everyone was busy all day.

The next day, Peace, Joy, and Merry tumbled from their bedrooms to get to the Christmas tree as fast as they could. Santa Clause had been there. He left a present for each of them.

All the little ones screamed at once, "Ahhhh, he's been here!"

When Mama and Papa got up, everyone sat around the fireplace. Papa read the Christmas story about Jesus' birth from the Bible.

After the story, everyone exchanged gifts.

Suddenly, Mama said, "I bet we're all hungry. You kids go out and play in the snow, and I'll get dinner ready." Soon, the smell of ham and potatoes drew the children inside.

Around the dinner table, they all enjoyed each other. After dinner, they sang Christmas carols and laughed. It was the best Christmas they had ever had.

The End

Chinese New Years

BY JESSICA, TIM, AND CODY

It was a cold January day. Ickchan Lee was playing noisily with her toy piano. "Stop making that racket!" demanded her mother. "Come with me and I will tell you about New Year's." So her mother put on her red coat and mittens. They took a walk to the store to get some food for New Year's dinner. They bought some New Year's dumplings and cakes. Ickchan Lee got an extra small cake for her grandma. She picked out the one with almonds on the top and cream in the middle. They finished buying the oranges, rice, and Ramen noodles. On the way home they stopped for the fireworks. Ickchan skipped along the sidewalk, singing.

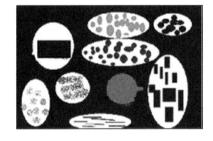

"This little frog has two eyes, four legs, one mouth, no tail, says croak, croak, and plops into the water."

When they got home her mother made paper fans, Chinese chews, and Chinese almond cookies. They decorated the house with paper lanterns. Ickchan Lee was in her traditional dress for the New Year's party.

They ate dumplings and cake. Ickchan Lee's mother showed her how to read the Chinese calendar. It was the Year of the Sheep. Happy New Year, Ickchan Lee!

Mama and Papa said to all the kids, "We might not have much money, but we sure do have a lot of love in our family." Everyone smiled. *The End*

Math Marvels

LINDA MCDONALD
    Katy Independent School District, Katy, Texas
    Used with permission of Katy ISD, Katy, Texas.

TYPE OF LESSON:	*Collaborative Project*
GRADE LEVEL:	*5–8*

The Evolution of Video Applications in Distance Education

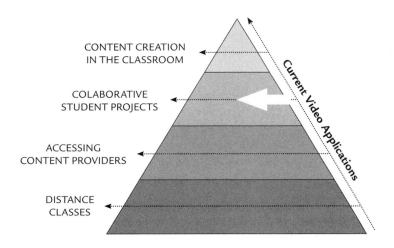

CORRELATION TO STANDARDS

Principles and Standards for School Mathematics

Problem Solving

Instructional programs from PK–12 should enable all students to:

NM-PROB.PK-12.2: Solve problems that arise in mathematics and in other contexts

NM-PROB.PK-12.3: Apply and adapt a variety of appropriate strategies to solve problems

NM-PROB.PK-12.4: Monitor and reflect on the process of mathematical problem solving

Reasoning and Proof

Instructional programs from PK–12 should enable all students to:

NM-PROB.REA.PK-12.1: Recognize reasoning and proof as fundamental aspects of mathematics

Communication

Instructional programs from PK–12 should enable all students to:

NM-PROB.COMM.PK-12.1: Organize and consolidate their mathematical thinking through communication

NM-PROB.COMM.PK-12.2: Communicate their mathematical thinking coherently and clearly to peers, teachers, and others

NM-PROB.COMM.PK-12.3: Analyze and evaluate the mathematical thinking and strategies of others;

NM-PROB.COMM.PK-12.4: Use the language of mathematics to express mathematical ideas precisely.

Connections

Instructional programs from PK–12 should enable all students to:

NM-PROB.CONN.PK-12.1: Recognize and use connections among mathematical ideas

NM-PROB.CONN.PK-12.2: Understand how mathematical ideas interconnect and build on one another to produce a coherent whole

NM-PROB.CONN.PK-12.3: Recognize and apply mathematics in contexts outside of mathematics

Representation

Instructional programs from PK–12 should enable all students to:

NM-PROB.REP.PK-12.1: Create and use representations to organize, record, and communicate mathematical ideas

NM-PROB.REP.PK-12.2: Select, apply, and translate among mathematical representations to solve problems

NM-PROB.REP.PK-12.3: Use representations to model and interpret physical, social, and mathematical phenomena

Reprinted with permission. © 2000 by the National Council of Teachers of Mathematics.

UNIT GOAL

To interact with others to use solution strategies to solve a problem and communicate the thinking process.

LESSON OBJECTIVES

After completing this lesson, students will be able to

- read a word problem and determine the question being asked,
- choose a solution strategy to solve a problem, and
- use math terms to communicate their thinking.

DURATION

45–60 minutes.

PRIOR KNOWLEDGE REQUIRED

Students should have an understanding of a variety of solution strategies, including drawing a picture, acting it out, making a chart, making it simpler, looking for a pattern, guessing and checking, working backward.

VOCABULARY

Words to be introduced through this lesson:

numerals
representation
solution
strategy

Pre-Conference Activities

Activity 1 • Problem-Solving Process and Strategies

Instructional Objective

Students participate in routine practice of problem-solving strategies.

Materials

In addition to classroom materials, these links may offer problems that can be used:

- www.eduplace.com/kids/mhm/
- http://school.discovery.com/brainboosters/
  (scroll down to Number and Math Play)
- www.Internet4classrooms.com/brain_teasers.htm *(list of links)*
- www.braingle.com/Math.html
- www.colstate.edu/mathcontest/
- http://nces.ed.gov/NCESKids/CRUNCH/challenge.asp
  (See the Mind Benders section)
- http://hlavolamy.szm.sk/brainteasers/puzzles-riddles.htm
- www.teachersfirst.com/twister/select.htm?CFID=399108&CFTOKEN=90794356

Procedure

The use of problem-solving strategies and the use of math language to communicate how solutions are derived should be integrated into all instructional units on a regular basis. This can be done in a variety of ways. Teachers should choose problems that best meet the needs of their classrooms.

Evaluation

The use of solution strategies is a developmental process. A grading rubric may be the most efficient assessment tool.

Activity 2 • Number of the Day/Math Jokes

Instructional Objective

Students solve problems with multiple solutions using all operations.

Materials

Math joke books

Procedure

1. A "number of the day" (e.g., "10") is chosen by the project facilitator or participating teachers and provided to each student group a few days before the videoconference.

2. Students write problems where the answer is the number of the day (e.g., the number of legs on a centipede divided by the number of toes on most people).

3. Student groups search for math jokes that can be shared.

Evaluation

Assess student work samples, completed problems, and student participation.

Preparation for Videoconference

- Overview of behavior expected during videoconference.

- Create and display a sign noting school name and location.

- Develop student questions. With your teacher partner for the videoconference, determine:

How you are going to get the problems together for the videoconference.

Option 1. You can work together on gathering four to five problems and develop one set of questions to share with the students. Both classes would then work on the same problem at a time during the videoconference.

Option 2. Each of you can develop your own four to five problems and each class would work on a different problem at the same time during the videoconference.

How you are going to share them with the students (i.e., in a PowerPoint presentation, on a document camera, on a paper document that is handed to each student).

Videoconference

Topic: *Math Marvels*

Participants: *Partner classrooms*

Introduction

Share sample "number of the day" problems (see Pre-Conference Activity 2). (10 minutes)

Activity and/or Presentation

The classroom teacher or facilitator (chosen by participating teachers prior to the session) actively directs the session and sets timelines for each problem step.

1. Students share their problems, one at a time.
2. Students are allowed think time to work with small group on site (on mute) for two to five minutes, depending on grade level and problem.
3. The teacher provides one to two hints to guide thinking and discussion.
4. Students share strategies with their partner class. Focus should be placed on the solution process *not* the answer.
5. The process is repeated for additional problems as time allows.
6. The session concludes with two to three math jokes from each site.

(30 minutes)

Post-Conference Activities

Follow-up Activity

Instructional Objective

Students will participate in routine practice of problem-solving strategies.

Materials

All problems that were presented to students during the videoconference session.

Procedure

1. Allow students to work with partners to complete problems as needed.
2. Students work in groups to resolve any unanswered questions about solutions.
3. Students could use the problem as a pattern for developing additional questions that could be used as an assessment.

Evaluation

Evaluate students on participation. Optional assessment of problem creation and solutions.

Mammals, Mammoths, Manatees!

KASEY GAYLORD
    Mote Marine Laboratory, SeaTrek Distance Learning, Sarasota, Florida
(www.seatrek.org)

TYPE OF LESSON:	*Content Provider*
GRADE LEVEL:	*5–8*

The Evolution of Video Applications in Distance Education

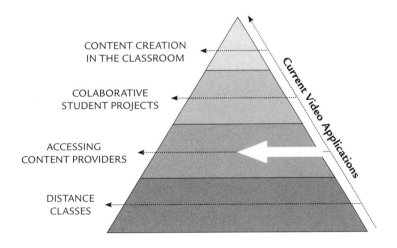

CORRELATION TO STANDARDS

National Science Education Standards

NS.5-8.3 Life Science

As a result of their activities in Grades 5–8, all students should develop understanding of:

- Structure and function in living systems
- Reproduction and heredity
- Regulation and behavior
- Populations and ecosystems
- Diversity and adaptations of organisms

NS.5-8.7 History and Nature of Science

As a result of activities in Grades 5–8, all students should develop understanding of:

- Science as a human endeavor
- Nature of science

Reprinted with permission. © 1995 by the National Academy of Sciences, Courtesy of the National Academies Press, Washington, D.C.

Principles and Standards for School Mathematics

Problem Solving

NM-PROB.PK-12.1: Build new mathematical knowledge through problem solving;

NM-PROB.PK-12.2: Solve problems that arise in mathematics and in other contexts;

NM-PROB.PK-12.3: Apply and adapt a variety of appropriate strategies to solve problems;

NM-PROB.PK-12.4: Monitor and reflect on the process of mathematical problem solving.

Reprinted with permission. © 2000 by the National Council of Teachers of Mathematics.

UNIT GOALS

- Students learn the basic anatomy and adaptations of manatees.
- Students learn what conservation measures are being taken to protect manatees.
- Students understand what captive-care requirements there are for manatees.
- Students design an environmental-enrichment device for manatees in captivity.

DURATION

Four to five 50-minute class periods. For the complete unit, please visit www.seatrek.org.

VOCABULARY

Words to be introduced through this lesson:

adaptation
captivity
conservation
extinct
hypothermia
mortality
paddle
pectoral flipper
sirenian
species
vibrissae

UNIT OVERVIEW

Florida manatees are marine mammals living along the coast of the southeastern United States. Although not terribly pretty, manatees are crucial to coastal habitats.

Manatees can grow to be up to 14-feet long and 3,000 pounds. Baby manatees, called calves, measure about 4-feet long and weigh about 30 pounds at birth.

Manatees have many adaptations that allow them to survive well in coastal habitats, whether it is fresh, brackish, or salt water. Protective oil glands near their eyes, fat to help retain body heat, and ability to replenish 90% of lung volume per breath, among many other adaptations, all allow the manatee to be the world's largest marine vegetarian.

UNIT PRE-QUESTIONS

1. What are manatees?
2. Why are they beneficial to coastal habitats?
3. What is an environmental enrichment device?

UNIT EVALUATION

Pre-test and post-test.

UNIT FOLLOW-UP DISCUSSION

1. What are some of the major adaptations manatees have for living in the water?
2. What are some of the causes for manatees being threatened or endangered?
3. What are environmental-enrichment devices? Why are they used?

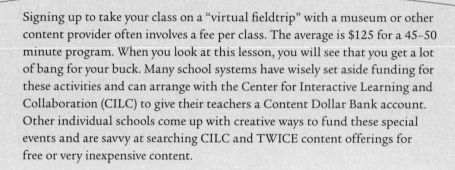

SPECIAL NOTE CONCERNING CONTENT PROVIDERS

Signing up to take your class on a "virtual fieldtrip" with a museum or other content provider often involves a fee per class. The average is $125 for a 45–50 minute program. When you look at this lesson, you will see that you get a lot of bang for your buck. Many school systems have wisely set aside funding for these activities and can arrange with the Center for Interactive Learning and Collaboration (CILC) to give their teachers a Content Dollar Bank account. Other individual schools come up with creative ways to fund these special events and are savvy at searching CILC and TWICE content offerings for free or very inexpensive content.

Pre-Conference Activities

Activity 1 • Manatee Anatomy

Instructional Objective
Students learn the basic anatomy of manatees.

Main Lesson Standard
Diversity and adaptations of organisms.

Time Required
One class period.

Materials
- Research materials, including Internet and print sources
- Manatee Pre/Post-Test and Answer Key
- Manatee Fact Sheet (for teacher)
- Make a Life-Sized Manatee worksheet
- Manatee Anatomy worksheet (one per student)
- Manatee Web worksheet (one per student)
- Manatee Mania! information sheet (one per student)
- Two 10-foot lengths of butcher paper

Procedure

1. Divide the students into several groups.

2. Have one group of students use the Make a Life-Sized Manatee worksheet to produce a full-sized picture of a manatee. If you have enough groups, have the students make three manatees that can be separately marked to show external anatomy, organs, and skeletal system (see step 4).

3. While one group is making the manatee, have the other groups research the anatomy of a manatee to decide what needs to be labeled once the manatee is complete.

4. Once the students finish making the full-sized manatee picture, have the other groups add the anatomical parts to it.

5. Have the students label their Manatee Anatomy worksheet to match the large copy.

6. Distribute the Manatee Mania! information sheet and the Manatee Web worksheet to the students. Have them begin filling out the Manatee Web worksheet with the information they have learned so far.

Evaluation

Teachers should use the Manatee Fact Sheet to check answers on this activity. Teachers may use the Manatee Pre/Post-Test to evaluate the students' learning outcomes.

Activity 2 • Manatee Adaptations

Instructional Objective

The student researches adaptations and then finds real-world alternatives.

Main Lesson Standard

Diversity and adaptations of organisms.

Time Required

One class period.

Materials

- Reference materials on manatees, including Internet and print sources
- Manatee Websites information sheet
- Manatee Adaptations worksheet
- Paper and writing instruments

Procedure

1. Go over the biological definition and concept of *adaptation* with your class. A useful definition of adaptation is: "An alteration or adjustment in structure or habits, often hereditary, by which a species or individual improves its condition in relationship to its environment" (Dictionary.com).

2. Have the students get into groups of three to four students.

3. Have the students research the adaptations of a manatee.

4. The students should come up with ways to show at least five special adaptations manatees have by using everyday items that humans use (e.g., manatees use their paddles like humans use flippers on their feet when swimming). Unless you choose to have them do so, the students do not have to collect the items and present them. You may also opt to limit the number of anatomical features listed to encourage the students to think of behavioral adaptations.

5. Have the students complete the Manatee Adaptations worksheet with their five adaptations, listing the equivalencies next to each manatee adaptation.

6. Have the groups present their ideas to the class. Have the students listen and include on their sheet any adaptations that they don't have on their list.

7. Have the students continue filling in the Manatee Web worksheet.

Evaluation

Teachers should use the Manatee Fact Sheet to check answers on this activity. Teachers may use the pre/post-test to evaluate the students' learning outcomes.

Preparation for Videoconference

- Overview behavior expectations during videoconference.

- Create and display a sign noting school name and location.

- Develop and write down student questions. Review the procedure for interaction with the class.

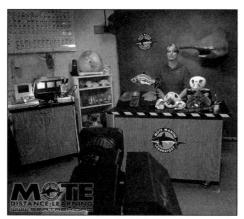

SeaTrek distance learning videoconference

Videoconference

Topic: *Mammals, Mammoths, Manatees!*

Content Provider: *Mote Marine Laboratory's SeaTrek Program*

SeaTrek videoconference in the classroom

Instructional Objective

Students learn how manatees are kept in captivity and about conservation efforts being done now to save the manatees.

Duration

One class period.

Main Lesson Standard

Structure and Function (NSES)

Materials

Manatee Web worksheet (from lesson 1) filled out by students

Activity and/or Presentation

During the videoconference, Mote Marine Laboratory presents a 50-minute media-rich videoconference on manatees. The topics covered in the videoconference include

- manatees in captivity,
- manatee training,
- environmental enrichment devices (EEDs),
- conservation issues with manatees, and
- instructions about how students can help manatee conservation.

Question/Answer or Discussion

Following the program students and teachers ask questions regarding this topic (10 minutes). The SeaTrek Educator answers the questions as thoroughly as possible and responds to as many questions as the allotted time allows. The teacher helps facilitate this discussion. Please keep in mind that students can interact with the SeaTrek Educator throughout the entire length of the program.

Post-Conference Activities

Follow-up Activity • Make a Manatee Toy

Instructional Objective

The student designs an environmental enrichment device (EED) that could be used with a manatee.

Time Required

One to two class periods.

Main Lesson Standard

Nature of Science (NSES).

Materials

- Internet access
- Drawing paper
- Crayons, colored pencils, markers, etc.
- Manatee environmental enrichment device idea form (one per student); using this form, students briefly describe their EED idea, list supplies needed, and give building directions. Students also attach a drawing of their EED.

Procedure

1. Ask students what they remember about an environmental enrichment device, as was shown in the videoconference.

2. Have students look at the following Mote Marine website to look at more EEDs and the requirements for EEDs:
   http://isurus.mote.org/~hughbuffett/pages/Help/help3.eed.phtml

3. Explain to students that their assignment is to develop an EED for Mote's manatees. Click on Photo Gallery of Manatees and Their Toys to see examples of current EEDs.

4. Have students describe and draw a picture of an EED of their own design. They should include a list of the things that are needed to make it (e.g., PVC pipe, etc.). They should complete the Manatee Environmental Enrichment Device Idea form.

5. Have students present their designs to the class.

6. If the teacher would like, have students vote on which design should be submitted to the Mote Marine website (http://isurus.mote.org/~hughbuffett/pages/formEED.html) for consideration by Mote Marine scientists.

Evaluation

Teachers may use the Manatee Pre/Post-Test to evaluate students' learning outcomes.

MAMMALS, MAMMOTHS, MANATEES!

Manatee Pre/Post-Test

_____ **1.** Characteristics of mammals include all of the following EXCEPT:

    A. giving live birth   C. having hair on their body

    B. breathing using gills   D. being warm-blooded

_____ **2.** An animal's diet is an important source of:

    A. air   C. energy

    B. carbon dioxide   D. genetics

_____ **3.** Manatees are related to:

    A. elephants   C. hyraxes

    B. aardvarks   D. all of the above

_____ **4.** A change in water temperature may cause animals to:

    A. move into an area   C. move away from an area

    B. die   D. all of the above are possible

_____ **5.** Because they eat only plants, manatees are considered to be:

    A. carnivores   C. herbivores

    B. omnivores   D. apex predators

_____ **6.** _____ are one of the biggest threats to manatee survival.

    A. toxic plants   C. hyraxes

    B. herbivores   D. speedboats

_____ **7.** Manatees share all the following characteristics with people EXCEPT:

    A. eyelids   C. an umbilicus

    B. fingernails   D. hair

_____ **8.** Adaptations to an environment increase the likelihood that the species will:

    A. survive   C. die back

    B. go extinct   D. starve

Manatee Pre/Post-Test *(Continued)*

_____ **9.** Scientists train captive manatees so that:

        A. information can be learned about the manatees

        B. the manatees do not get bored

        C. the manatees do not get fat

        D. there is no danger to the scientists working with them

_____ **10.** Manatees can remain submerged for up to:

        A. 1 hour   C. 45 minutes

        B. 20 minutes   D. 30 minutes

MAMMALS, MAMMOTHS, MANATEES!

Manatee Pre/Post-Test Answer Key

Teachers: Please do NOT go over correct answers with students after the pre-test.

1. B
2. C
3. D
4. D
5. C
6. D
7. A
8. A
9. A
10. B

MAMMALS, MAMMOTHS, MANATEES!

Manatee Fact Sheet

Sources: *Sea World, Save the Manatee Club, Florida Marine Research Institute*

Classification

- Modern manatees have been in Florida for more than 1 million years.

- Manatees are in the order Sirenia and the family Trichechidae.

  - *Trichechus manatus,* the West Indian manatee: There are two subspecies of the West Indian manatee: the Florida manatee (*Trichechus manatus latirostris*) and the Antillean manatee (*Trichechus manatus manatus*). These subspecies are distinguished by certain cranial features and by their geographical distribution.

  - *Trichechus senegalensis,* the West African manatee: About the same size and shape as the West Indian manatee, the West African manatee differs in some important respects: its eyes, snout, and cranial bones are different.

  - *Trichechus inunguis,* the Amazonian manatee: The Amazonian manatee is the smallest of the manatees. Several physical characteristics distinguish it from the other two species.

- Even though the oldest known Sirenian fossils were found in Jamaica, it is likely that Sirenians originated in Eurasia or Africa. During the Middle Eocene period (45–50 million years ago), the ancestors of manatees probably reached South America.

- Fossils exist for more than a dozen Sirenian species; only five species have been extant during the time of man; only four are extant today.

- Studies using biochemical analysis of proteins show that the closest modern relatives of sirenians are elephants, aardvarks, and small mammals known as hyraxes.

Habitat and Distribution

- All species except the Amazonian manatee can live in salt, brackish, or fresh water.

- They prefer water above 70 degrees and will risk hypothermia if in water less than 60 degrees.

- They may be found in any waterway 3.25 feet or deeper but are usually close to land; they are usually not in water more than 15 feet deep.

Anatomical and Physiological Characteristics

- Can remain submerged for 20 minutes.

- Heart rate: 50–60 beats per minute.

- No leg bones or pelvis—have a tiny L-shaped bone embedded in the muscle.

- Average size: 10 feet, 1,200 lbs. Record size: 13.5-foot pregnant female, 3,750 lbs.

- Marine mammals stop bleeding in water due to a special clotting mechanism.

- Body temperature is 95.7° Fahrenheit.

Manatee Fact Sheet *(Continued)*

- Skin can be up to 2 inches thick and cannot be pierced by arrows.
- Bones are heavy and solid (no marrow); red blood cells are produced in the spinal column.
- Have fingernails.
- Only six cervical (neck) vertebrae; cannot turn head.
- Continue to grow throughout their lives.
- Females are generally larger than males.
- Digestive and respiratory systems are not connected.
- The two small pectoral flippers on a manatee's upper body are used for steering or walking along the bottom, not swimming.
- Scientists think manatees do not have vocal cords.
- Manatees do not have eyelashes.
- Can move one side of lip pads independently of the other side.
- Barnacles can attach themselves to manatees in salt water, but they die and drop off when manatees return to fresh water.
- Diaphragm pushes outward toward lungs, not upward. Only mammal, as far as we know, in which the diaphragm does not touch the sternum; it is attached instead to a vertebra in the thorax.
- Scientists determine a manatee's age by counting the growth rings in its ear bone.

Senses

- Manatees possess the ability to have smell markers, using rub spots (message centers).
- Vibrissae (whiskers) are very sensitive; outer ones more so than inner ones.
- Have same taste flavor sensors we do.
- Cannot smell underwater, but we think they can above water.
- Skin is very sensitive and often manatees will touch each other.
- Hairs are about an inch apart—don't provide warmth but are used to detect changes in water currents.
- Manatees close eyes with a sphincter muscle.
- Can see easily at a distance but do not have good depth perception at short range.
- Studies on manatee food preferences at Blue Springs, Florida, indicate that manatees avoid certain plants that contain toxins.

Adaptations

- Gland next to the eyes produces a special oil to coat the eye and protect it from salt
- Manatees have a low metabolism, one of the lowest of all mammals.

Manatee Fact Sheet *(Continued)*

- Can fast (go long periods without eating)— Florida manatees for up to a month; Amazonian manatees for 6 months
- Being so big is a heat-saving adaptation.
- 20% of weight is fat.
- Heart beats slower while diving (30 beats per minute during an 8-minute dive).
- Can dive up to 30 feet, but usually not more than 10 feet.
- Can renew up to 90% of oxygen in lungs with each breath (humans renew only 10%).

Behavior

- Some travel as far as 30 miles a day.
- Sometimes groan when they stretch.
- They are endogenous (don't keep a normal schedule of waking and sleeping).
- Usually solitary, but when they are together in warm-water refuges they have constant body contact.
- When in a herd, manatees will rise and breathe in unison.
- Feed 6–8 hours per day.
- Rest 2–12 hours per day.

Diet and Eating Habits

- Food takes about 7 days to move through digestive tract.
- Chew two times a second.
- Eat 4–15% of body weight daily in the wild.
- Huge molars have no roots but are held in place by ligaments.
- One of two mammals that have an unending supply of teeth (shares distinction with a species of kangaroo).
- They crop overhanging branches, consume acorns, and haul themselves partially out of the water to eat bank vegetation.
- Most digestion takes place in large intestine, as in elephants and horses.
- Have 24 to 32 molars.
- Feed on more than 60 species of plants.

Reproduction

- Females are sexually mature at 7–8 years of age and bear young the rest of their lives.
- No fixed breeding season.
- Males mature at 9–10 years of age.
- Breed year-round.

Manatee Fact Sheet *(Continued)*

Birth and Care of Young

- 13-month pregnancy, giving birth to one to two young; nurse for 2 years
- Newborn calves average 4 feet in length and 60–70 pounds.
- Calves' teeth don't start moving forward until the calf begins eating plants.
- Most Florida manatees are born in spring and summer.

Communication

- Emit sounds when frightened, sexually aroused, or interacting with each other.
- Mothers respond to their calves from more than 200 feet away when the calf squeals.

Longevity and Causes of Death

- Manatees probably live 50–60 years, but no one knows for sure. One-third of all deaths are from speedboats and crushing injuries.
- Watercraft-related mortality is the leading cause of death in adult manatees.
- Natural causes of death include cold weather, diseases, and parasites
- Human-related causes of death include pollution, poaching, harassment, watercraft accidents, habitat destruction, floodgates and navigation locks, and accidental entanglement.

Conservation

- Recent research conducted at the Florida Marine Research Institute revealed that of the manatees whose carcasses had been recovered in the salvage program, few were living past the age of 30, and the majority of animals died between birth and 10 years of age, nowhere near their estimated life expectancy of 60 years.
- The biggest threat is the destruction of the sea-grass beds where they feed.
- All species are protected by national or local laws and agreements:
  - Marine Mammal Protection Act of 1972
  - Endangered Species Act of 1973
  - Florida Manatee Sanctuary Act of 1978
  - The Convention on International Trade of Endangered Species

Wow! Facts

- Manatees are only marine mammal that eats plants.
- Largest vegetarian creature in the sea.
- Bigger than any land animal in the United States.

MAMMALS, MAMMOTHS, MANATEES!

Manatee Mania!

Fun facts about the world's largest marine vegetarian!

Would you believe...

- Studies show that the closest modern relatives of manatees and dugongs aren't dolphins or whales but elephants, aardvarks, and small mammals known as hyraxes!

- Manatees can remain submerged for up to 20 minutes!

- Manatees can renew up to 90% of the oxygen in their lungs with each breath (compared to only 10% in humans)!

- A manatee's heart beats slower when it's diving—down to 30 beats per minute during an 8-minute dive!

- 20% of a manatee's body weight is fat!

- Manatees probably live 50–60 years, but no one knows for sure!

Chew on this...

- Manatees can haul themselves partially out of the water to eat bank vegetation!

- Manatees in the wild can eat up to 15% of their body weight daily!

- The largest manatee ever recorded was a pregnant female: 13.5 feet long and weighing 3,750 pounds!

Manatees have...

- Fingernails!

- Hair that can detect water currents!

- Special glands to coat and protect the eyes from salt!

- An unending supply of teeth!

Whoa!

- One-third of all manatee deaths are from speedboats and crushing injuries!

- Watercraft-related mortality is the leading cause of death in adult manatees!

MAMMALS, MAMMOTHS, MANATEES!

Manatee Websites

Mote Marine Laboratory's Hugh and Buffett
http://isurus.mote.org/~hughbuffett/pages/About/about1.hb.phtml

Florida Marine Research Institute
www.floridamarine.org/features/default.asp?id=1001

Save the Manatee Club
www.savethemanatee.org

Sea World—Manatee information pages
www.seaworld.org/infobooks/manatee/home.html

Florida Fish and Wildlife Conservation Commission—Manatee Program
http://myfwc.com/manatee/

UNEP Carribean Environment Programme—Manatees and Dugongs
www.cep.unep.org/kids/kids.html

Enchanted Learning—All About Manatees
www.enchantedlearning.com/subjects/mammals/manatee/

MAMMALS, MAMMOTHS, MANATEES!

Make a Life-Sized Manatee!

Directions

Use the scale on this manatee to make a life-sized manatee.

Scale (in inches) 1:24

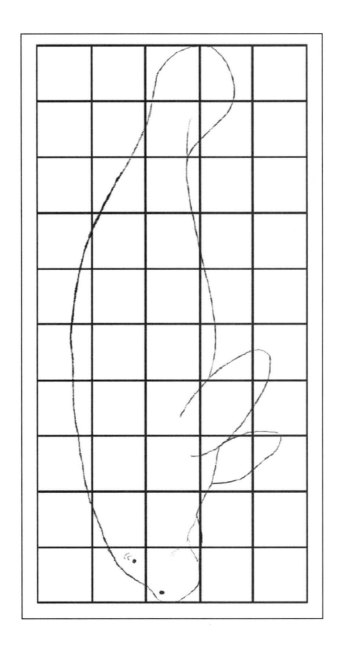

MAMMALS, MAMMOTHS, MANATEES!

Manatee Anatomy

Instructions

Label this manatee with the parts labeled on the life-sized manatee.

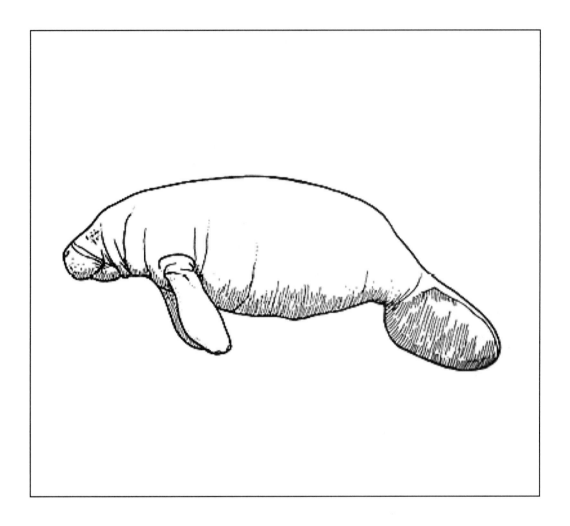

MAMMALS, MAMMOTHS, MANATEES!

Manatee Web

Instructions

Write in the information about Florida manatees.

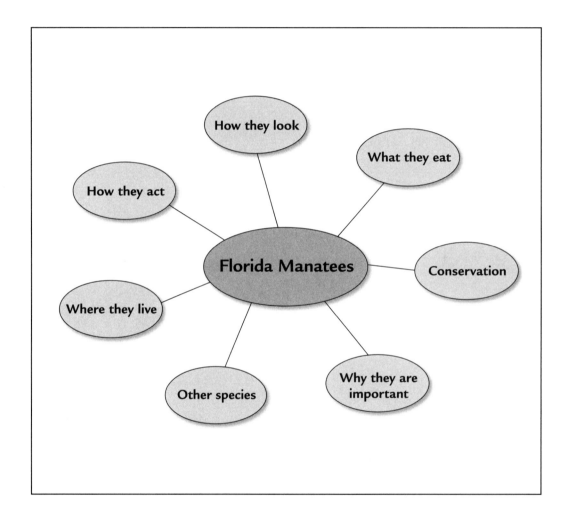

MAMMALS, MAMMOTHS, MANATEES!

Manatee Adaptations

Instructions

Find at least five adaptations that manatees have. Draw a line to where the adaptation is on the manatee.

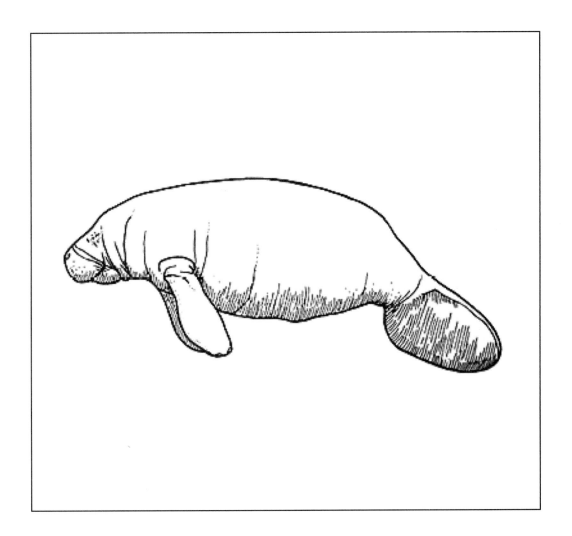

Genocide Study

EDYE CAINE, Humanities Chairperson 6-12
    Lakeland Central School District, Shrub Oak, New York

JOHN BLASER, Technology Integration Specialist
    Eastchester UFSD, Eastchester, New York

TYPE OF LESSON:	*Content Experts*
GRADE LEVEL:	*6–8*

The Evolution of Video Applications in Distance Education

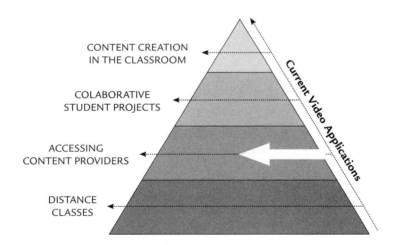

CORRELATION TO STANDARDS

National Standards for History—World History

NSS-WH.5-12.9 ERA 9: The 20th Century Since 1945: Promises and Paradoxes

The student in grades 5–12 should understand:

- major global trends since World War II.

National Geography Standards

NSS-G.K-12.2 Places and Regions

As a result of their activities in grades K–12, all students should:

- Understand the physical and human characteristics of places

- Understand that people create regions to interpret Earth's complexity

- Understand how culture and experience influence people's perceptions of places and regions

NSS-G.K-12.4 Human Systems

As a result of their activities in grades K–12, all students should:

- Understand the characteristics, distribution, and migration of human populations on Earth's surface

- Understand the characteristics, distribution, and complexity of Earth's cultural mosaics

- Understand the patterns and networks of economic interdependence on Earth's surface

- Understand the processes, patterns, and functions of human settlement

- Understand how the forces of cooperation and conflict among people influence the division and control of Earth's surface

UNIT GOALS

- Provide a live educational experience for students to work with and learn from experts in the field of genocide.

- Enable students to work collaboratively around the world to promote tolerance and understanding.

LESSON OBJECTIVES

After completing this lesson, students will be able to

- read, write, listen, and speak for information and understanding;

- read, write, listen, and speak for literary response and expression;

- read, write, listen, and speak for critical analysis and evaluation; and

- read, write, listen, and speak for social interaction.

In addition, students will be able to use a variety of intellectual skills to

- demonstrate their understanding of major ideas, eras, themes, developments, and turning points in world history and to examine the broad sweep of history from a variety of perspectives;

- demonstrate their understanding of the geography of the interdependent world in which we live—local, national, and global—including the distribution of people, places, and environments over Earth's surface; and

- demonstrate their understanding of how the United States and other societies develop economic systems and associated institutions to allocate scarce resources, how major decision-making units function in the United States and other national economies, and how an economy solves the scarcity problem through market and non-market mechanisms.

DURATION

Five weeks.

PRIOR KNOWLEDGE REQUIRED

Students should have an understanding of

- geographical locations of the countries, and

- basic research strategies.

VOCABULARY

Words to be introduced through this lesson:

Bosnia
Cambodia
Declaration of Human Rights
genocide
humanitarian
Hutu
Janjaweed
Khmer Rouge
Rwanda
Sudan
tribunal
Tutsi
Uganda
United Nations

Pre-Conference Activities

Activity 1 • Genocide Watch

Instructional Objective

Students are able to define the term genocide and understand the eight stages of genocide as defined by Gregory H. Stanton of Genocide Watch.

Materials

- "What Is Genocide?" article, printed from www.genocidewatch.org/whatisgenocide.htm.

- "The 8 Stages of Genocide" article by Gregory H. Stanton, printed from www.genocidewatch.org/8stages.htm.

  ("The 8 Stages of Genocide" was originally written in 1996 at the U.S. Department of State and was presented at the Yale University Center for International and Area Studies in 1998.)

Procedure

1. Have students read the article "What Is Genocide?" as a homework assignment. The next day in class, lead students in a Socratic seminar to help them gain a genuine understanding of the term.

2. Have students read the article "The 8 Stages of Genocide." Have them discuss, together as a group, the various stages and create a template for future research. Students will be able to use the template to determine whether topics and events studied are considered to be acts of genocide.

Evaluation

Creation of template as well as use of template throughout research portion of the project.

Activity 2 • Analyzing Genocide

Instructional Objective

Students are able to critically analyze events that occurred in Cambodia, Bosnia, Rwanda, and the Sudan to determine whether acts of genocide were committed based on the templates created in Activity 1.

Materials

- Books offering historical perspectives on the four countries, Internet resources, live videoconferences with experts.

- Convention on the Prevention and Punishment of the Crime of Genocide (www.preventgenocide.org/law/convention/text.htm)

- Research Guidelines handout. This handout includes protocols for student research and provide students with steps necessary to be successful in their research. This handout should also highlight valuable resources. The following is an example of items included in the handout.

Procedure

1. Develop questions to guide your research.

2. Research genocide as it applies to your assigned country.

3. Bring your questions to your assigned videoconference.

Helpful hints...

- Use the *Convention on the Prevention and Punishment of the Crime of Genocide* definition of genocide as a basis for all research.

- Access library databases as well as pre-selected links off the Social Studies webpage as resources for information.

- Read and highlight the information.

- Use a research journal to compile your data.

- Evaluate the data collected.

- Create a list of questions you have to ask the expert about genocide in your selected country.

- Utilize the wikispace as a means of communicating with other students researching your assigned country. It is always helpful to bat ideas off of others to gain insight and perspective!

Procedure

1. Give students time in the library for research.

2. Students will collect data, critically analyze the data, formulate questions for the experts, and ultimately apply the information to the template on genocide as they decide for themselves whether the specific events should be considered acts of genocide.

Evaluation

Students will propose their original ideas on the genocide determination of an event in an in-class essay assignment.

Preparation for Videoconference

- Review behavior expectations during videoconference.

- Create and display a sign noting school name and location.

- Develop and write down student questions. Review the procedure for interaction with the class.

Videoconference

Topic: *Genocide*

Content Providers: *Gregory Stanton, Director of Genocide Watch (Cambodia, Rwanda)*

Colin Thomas-Jensen, International Crisis Group (Sudan)

Julia Speigel, Policy Analyst, ENOUGH Project (Uganda)

Elvir Camdzic, Director of Government Relations, Bosnian American Advisory Council (Bosnia)

Alan Moskin, World War II veteran (Germany)

Clara Knopfler, Holocaust survivor, Auschwitz (Germany)

Introduction

Mike Griffith of Global-Leap, based in the U.K., serves as the moderator of the videoconference. Each expert is introduced to the students, and a brief biography of each individual is presented. (*Please note:* Each videoconference covers one country.)

Activity and/or Presentation

Each expert provides a general overview of the country they are speaking on. They specifically address acts of genocide within those countries. Students from each site then have the opportunity to ask questions of the experts. These can be questions previously researched and planned or impromptu questions as a result of the presentation. Students also have the opportunity to ask questions of each other at the end of the conference.

Question/Answer or Discussion

After the expert completes the general overview, he or she turns it over to the students for their questions (10–15 minutes). Mike Griffith then turns to each of the sites for further questions or comments from the students. If a site is not ready at that time, Mike moves the discussion along and returns at a later time. Each site has at least two separate opportunities to pose questions of the experts. At the end of the conference, Mike asks for closing comments or reflections from each of the sites.

Genocide study videoconference

Post-Conference Activities

Follow-up Activity

Instructional Objective

Students are able to apply the concepts learned from the unit and devise and implement their own programs addressing genocide around the world.

Materials

Students are provided with a list of possible projects including, but certainly not limited to,

- creating a website for educational purposes,
- starting a letter-writing campaign,
- volunteering for a human rights organization,
- organizing a vigil, or
- organizing a school assembly addressing the topic of genocide.

Procedure

1. The teacher creates a wikispace, gathers the e-mail addresses of the students and invites them to participate. Students are required to post to their assigned topics through the wiki. All students can move freely throughout the wiki and participate in the general discussion boards. Students usually find it helpful to bat ideas off of others to gain insight and perspective.

2. Each student is assigned a country. Students use the wikispace to communicate with other students researching the same assigned country.

3. Students work as a cohesive group to design and implement a project that will ultimately help to better the lives of refugees in that country.

4. Students present their project at a final videoconference.

Evaluation

Assessment of final project as per rubric.

Chapter 4

High School Lessons

Employability Skills and Distance Learning
Michigan Students Come to Ohio

JOANN SANTILLO, Technology Integration Specialist
    Mahoning County Career and Technical Center, Canfield, Ohio

TYPE OF LESSON:	*Collaborative Project*
GRADE LEVEL:	*11–12*

The Evolution of Video Applications in Distance Education

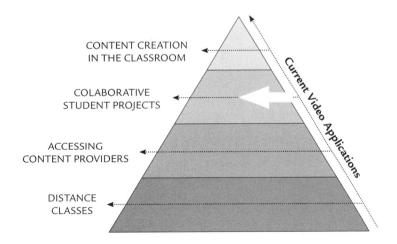

CORRELATION TO STANDARDS

National Educational Technology Standards

6. **Technology Operations and Concepts**

   Students demonstrate a sound understanding of technology concepts, systems, and operations. Students:

   a. understand and use technology systems

   b. select and use applications effectively and productively

   c. troubleshoot systems and applications

   d. transfer current knowledge to the learning of new technologies

Standards for the English Language Arts

NL-ENG.K-12.4 Communication Skills

Students adjust their use of spoken, written, and visual language (e.g., conventions, style, vocabulary) to communicate effectively with a variety of audiences and for different purposes.

NL-ENG.K-12.5 Communication Strategies

Students employ a wide range of strategies as they write and use different writing process elements appropriately to communicate with different audiences for a variety of purposes.

NL-Eng.K-12.7 Evaluating Data

Students conduct research on issues and interests by generating ideas and questions, and by posing problems. They gather, evaluate, and synthesize data from a variety of sources (e.g., print and nonprint texts, artifacts, people) to communicate their discoveries in ways that suit their purpose and audience.

NL-Eng. K-12.12 Applying Language Skills

Students use spoken, written, and visual language to accomplish their own purposes (e.g., for learning, enjoyment, persuasion, and the exchange of information).

Reprinted with permission. © 1996 by the International Reading Association and the National Council of Teachers of English. Available at www.ncte.org/standards/.

UNIT GOAL

Students gain valuable knowledge of the job application and interview process.

LESSON OBJECTIVES

After completing this lesson, students will be able to

- acquire and publish information in a variety of media formats,
- incorporate communication design principles in their work,

- use technology to disseminate information to multiple audiences and use tele-communication tools to interact with others,

- collaborate in real time with individuals and groups who are located in different schools and states, and

- participate in distance education opportunities that expand academic offerings and enhance learning.

DURATION

15 class periods.

PRIOR KNOWLEDGE REQUIRED

Students should have an understanding of

- skills needed in the clerical workforce;

- job applications and resumes, how to complete them, and what makes them good or bad;

- questions an interviewer may ask; and

- Microsoft Publisher program.

VOCABULARY

Words to be introduced through this lesson:

application blank
articulation
collaborate
diction
distance learning
employability skills
ice breakers
job description
rating sheet
real-time
resume
videoconference

Background

Michigan, like other states, is trying to prepare students for jobs through employability programs; but what they are finding is that they don't take the instructors seriously when it comes to the interview process. So Michigan's Galien High School and our school, Mahoning County Career and Technical Center, in Canfield, Ohio, decided to try a different approach for the application and interview process, using videoconferencing.

Through a series of e-mails, teachers from both schools developed the format of the distance-learning project. Students at the near site (Ohio school) developed a company for which they created job vacancies. They advertised at the far site (Michigan school), and students there submitted their applications and resumes for the vacancies. The near-site students selected several final candidates, who were then interviewed via videoconference. The Michigan school videotaped the interviews for later viewing and evaluation.

Pre-Conference Activities

Activity 1 • Job Search

Instructional Objective

Students work in cooperative groups and develop the job-related materials that will enable the far-site students to complete an application process and apply for position openings.

Materials

- Computer and printer
- Software programs: Microsoft Word and Publisher
- Paper

Procedure

1. The teacher and students brainstorm to create a fictitious company and its organizational chart (using Microsoft Word). Using Microsoft Publisher, students create a flyer that advertises the company. The flyer must include, but is not limited to: (a) name, address, and phone number of company, (b) brief description of the company, and (c) services the company offers.

2. Students create a company letterhead using Microsoft Publisher or Word. The company letterhead includes, but is not limited to: (a) name, address, and phone number of company, (b) appropriate graphic. (Duration: one class period.)

3. Students create two fliers, using Microsoft Publisher, that announce the two position openings: one for a clerical position, and one for a data entry position. The fliers are required to include the following: (a) position, (b) duties, (c) qualifications, (d) salary, and (e) person to respond to.

4. Students develop an application form to be sent to the far-site students. The position openings and the application blank are e-mailed to the far-site school.

Evaluation

The class discusses and critiques the work produced and receives teacher approval before sending the material to the far-site students.

Activity 2 • Job Interview

Instructional Objective

To help prepare for the upcoming interview videoconference, students participate in a preliminary get-acquainted videoconference with a planned structured icebreaker activity planned by the far-site students.

Materials

Videoconference equipment

Procedure

1. Near-site and far-site students introduce themselves by using the following icebreaker: Students tell their first name and describe themselves in one word (e.g., My name is Joe and I am jolly). (Duration: one class period.)

2. If time permits, students tell a little about their course and school.

Evaluation

After the videoconference has ended, a blog will be set up for both schools, and students will have the opportunity to evaluate the project. Some of the questions posed on the blog are as follows:

(a) What did you like or dislike about the project and why? (b) Did you take the interview process seriously—why or why not? (c) What was it like to meet other students on camera? (d) What would you like to see changed or added to this project? (e) Would you suggest that we do this videoconference project with next year's class—why or why not? (f) How did you feel being interviewed by someone on camera, rather than in person?

Activity 3 • Job Interview Skills

Instructional Objective

Students are able to identify behaviors and attitudes valued by employers, evaluate and critique resumes and applications, and select appropriate candidates to be interviewed.

Materials

Resumés and applications from far-site students.

Procedure

1. After receiving the resumés and applications sent by far-site students, near-site students discuss and critique them as to neatness and completeness and then select the far-site candidates (total of 12) that will be interviewed. After the selection, they notify the far-site teacher, and the teacher informs the 12 candidates to be interviewed. (Duration: two class periods.)

2. Organize interview: (a) determine who will be doing the interview), (b) research on the Internet and compile a list of interview questions for the videoconference, and (c) create an interview rating form that will be used during the videoconference. (Duration: three class periods.)

Evaluation

The class discusses and critiques the work produced, revises if needed, and gets teacher approval.

Preparation for Videoconference

The following tasks are completed to prepare for the videoconference:

- Review behavior expectations for the videoconference. Since the interview videoconference will be conducted just like an actual interview, appropriate dress and behavior are required.

- Create and display a sign noting school name and location.

- Have interviewers display the appropriate school banner in the background.

- Develop student questions: Students in near site develop specific interview questions. They enlist the help of two faculty members to conduct the interviews with the far-site students.

Videoconference

Topic: *Employability Skills (Interview)*

Participants: *Mahoning County Career and Technical Center (Ohio) and Galien High School (Michigan)*

Introduction

After a series of communications between the two schools, the actual Interview Day Videoconference is held. The far-site school sends the near-site school an interview schedule with the names and times of the students who will be interviewed. Two faculty members from the near-site school conduct the videoconference interviews with the far-site students. Each candidate is rated on an interview form prepared by the near-site school. Interviews are 10 minutes each. (Duration: two class periods.)

Activity and/or Presentation

The interviews are conducted within a 15-minute block of time. Each candidate is given 10 minutes for the actual interview. Five minutes in between interviews gives the interviewers time to complete the rating sheet and time to have the next candidate come in to be interviewed.

After all the students are interviewed, the interview rating sheets are mailed back to the far-site students.

Interview day videoconference

Post-Conference Activities

Follow-up Activity

Instructional Objective

Students are able to evaluate the employability skills lesson and communicate their ideas and suggestions in a positive manner.

Materials

Computer

Duration

One class period.

Procedure

The near-site class is divided into groups and creates a PowerPoint presentation illustrating some of the highlights of the project. A rubric is used to evaluate the PowerPoint presentations. One presentation is to be presented for the follow-up videoconference.

Evaluation

Conduct a follow-up videoconference with both schools and critique the interview project and discuss some of the blog entries from each school.

Summary Comments from Teachers

This videoconference provides an opportunity for students from two different states to work and learn from each other, meet deadlines, and practice public speaking skills. It also provides a different approach to practicing interviews; students took it more seriously.

Water Usage in Your Family

TYPE OF LESSON:	*Content Expert*
GRADE LEVEL:	*9–12*

The Evolution of Video Applications in Distance Education

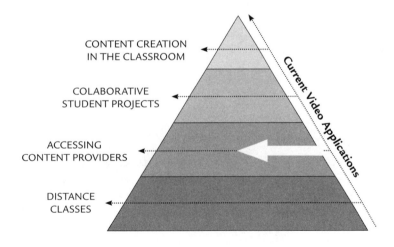

CONTENT CREATION IN THE CLASSROOM

COLABORATIVE STUDENT PROJECTS

ACCESSING CONTENT PROVIDERS

DISTANCE CLASSES

Current Video Applications

CORRELATION TO STANDARDS

Principles and Standards for School Mathematics

Number and Operations

Instructional programs from PK–12 should enable all students to:

NM-NUM.9-12.3: Compute fluently and make reasonable estimates

In Grades 9–12 all students should:

- develop fluency in operations with real numbers, vectors, and matrices, using mental computation or paper-and-pencil calculations for simple cases and technology for more-complicated cases

- judge the reasonableness of numerical computations and their results

Connections

Instructional programs from PK–12 should enable all students to:

NM-PROB.CONN.PK-12.2: Understand how mathematical ideas interconnect and build on one another to produce a coherent whole

NM-PROB.CONN.PK-12.3: Recognize and apply mathematics in contexts outside of mathematics

Reprinted with permission. © 2000 by the National Council of Teachers of Mathematics.

UNIT GOALS

- To gain a better understanding of how math may be applied to a real-world problem.

- To create formulas in Excel using addition, multiplication, and percentage functions.

- To gain experience with videoconferencing as a form of content delivery.

LESSON OBJECTIVES

Students will be prepared to research comparative statistics and prepare a spreadsheet that calculates those statistics in meaningful, accurate, and easy to read formats for residential consumers, commercial customers, and supplier audiences.

DURATION

Pre-conference activity: one class period.

Videoconference: one class period.

Post-conference activity: one class period.

PRIOR KNOWLEDGE REQUIRED

Students should be familiar with:

- how to create formulas in Excel or another spreadsheet software.

- videoconferencing etiquette, including how to ask questions.

RESOURCES

- Computers with Excel or other spreadsheet software; at least one computer for every four students.

- Websites showing household water usage statistics; a good example is http://ga.water.usgs.gov/edu/sq3.html.

- An expert in water usage and water conservation strategies.

Pre-Conference Activities

Activity 1 • Understanding Water Usage

Instructional Objective

Students research household water usage statistics and prepare a spreadsheet that calculates water usage for a given household.

Procedure

In groups of four, students brainstorm all the ways an average household of four uses water on an average Saturday when everyone is at home. Students send the teacher their responses via a classroom connection tool, and the teacher compiles a list.

In groups, students use the Internet to research water usage statistics, finding average numbers of gallons of water used for each activity on the compiled list. Students should note the sources they use and cite them on the spreadsheet they will create.

Students create a spreadsheet that lists the various brainstormed activities that use water. Using their research, they create formulas that will calculate gallons of water used for each activity, for a family of four.

The teacher visits each group and has the group explain how they created each formula.

The teacher uses a projector or teacher/connection program to illustrate to students the various formulas that were created. Through consensus, the class determines what the best formula is to use.

Students return to their work using the final formula to calculate total water used for all activities. As a class, students discuss their results to make sure every group's spreadsheet is returning reasonable amounts. Are students surprised at how much water a family of four uses in one day?

As homework, the students will prepare a letter inviting an expert in the field of water management to join them as a class. (Although this will have been pre-arranged, a secondary cross-curricular activity can be injected into the unit.) Additionally, students should reach prepare 3–4 questions that they plan on asking during the question/answer period of the videoconference.

Preparation for Videoconference

- Overview behavioral expectations for students during videoconference.
- Create and display a sign noting school name and location.
- Develop student questions (be sure to write them out and review with class the procedure for interaction).

Videoconference

Topic: *Discussion with a Water Usage Expert*

Content provider: *Contact a local college/university or public works department to find an expert knowledgable about ways to conserve water at home. Before the videoconference, provide the expert with the class's compiled list of water-consuming household activities and ask him or her to discuss water conservation strategies and provide information on percentage reductions in water use for each strategy.*

Introduction

Ten minutes prior to program start, check video and audio, and remind students of proper videoconference etiquette.

Start time: Introduction of students and expert.

Activity and/or Presentation

(35 minutes)

The expert speaks about water usage and different ways everyday people may conserve water at home, noting the percentage reduction in water use for each strategy. Students take notes.

Question/Answer or Discussion

(15 minutes)

Students are given time to ask questions. Each student group should have the opportunity to ask at least one question.

Post-Conference Activity

Follow-up Activity

Instructional Objective

Using what they have learned from the videoconference and the spreadsheet they have already created, students re-calculate gallons of water saved by water conservation strategies.

Procedure

In groups, students return to their spreadsheets. For each activity, in new columns, students list a water use reduction strategy for that activity and note the percentage reduction in water used. Students are challenged to accomplish three things:

1. Create new formulas for each activity that reflect that amount of water used if the water use reduction strategy is implemented.

2. Create a new formula to calculate the new, reduced total amount of water used for all activities combined.

3. Create a new formula to calculate how many gallons of water were saved overall.

Students compare their results and reflect on what they have learned about using math in an everyday situation.

Optional Homework

Students write a paragraph (Grades 9–10) or essay (Grades 11–12) on how residential consumers, commercial consumers and suppliers can best utilize the information for enhancing their own environments.

Science

Troubled Waters

PAUL HIERONYMUS, Curriculum Technology Coordinator
Avon Local Schools, Avon, Ohio

TYPE OF LESSON:	*Content Expert, Collaborative Project*
GRADE LEVEL:	*10–12*

The Evolution of Video Applications in Distance Education

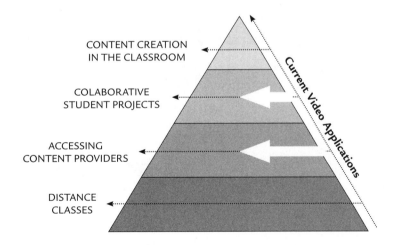

CORRELATION TO STANDARDS

National Science Education Standards

NS.K-4.1 Science as Inquiry

As a result of activities in Grades 9–12, all students should develop:

- Abilities necessary to do scientific inquiry

- Understanding about scientific inquiry

NS.9–12.2 Physical science

As a result of their activities in grades 9–12, all students should develop an understanding of

- Motions and forces

- Conservation of energy and increase in disorder

- Interactions of energy and matter

NS.9–12.6 Personal and social perspectives

As a result of activities in grades 9-12, all students should develop an understanding of

- Personal and community health

- Population growth

- Natural resources

- Environmental quality

- Natural and human-induced hazards

- Science and technology in local, national, and global challenges

NSS-G.K–12.1 The world in spatial terms

As a result of activities in grades K–12, all students should

- Understand how to use maps and other geographic representations, tools, and technologies to acquire, process, and report information from a spatial perspective.

- Understand how to use mental maps to organize information about people, places, and environments in a spatial context.

- Understand how to analyze the spatial organization of people, places, and environments on Earth's surface.

Reprinted with permission. © 1995 by the National Academy of Sciences, Courtesy of the National Academies Press, Washington, D.C.

Principles and Standards for School Mathematics

NM-DATA.9-12.3

Develop and evaluate inferences and predictions that are based on data

- use simulations to explore the variability of sample statistics from a known population and to construct sampling distributions;

- understand how sample statistics reflect the values of population parameters and use sampling distributions as the basis for informal inference;
- evaluate published reports that are based on data by examining the design of the study, the appropriateness of the data analysis, and the validity of conclusions;
- understand how basic statistical techniques are used to monitor process characteristics in the workplace.

Reprinted with permission. © 2000 by the National Council of Teachers of Mathematics.

UNIT GOALS

- To gain a better understanding of how changes made in the environment affect their community or sounding areas.
- To be able to work in groups to solve an environmental problem.
- To be able to solve real-world problems using data supplied by a professional organization and found through research.

LESSON OBJECTIVE

After completing this lesson, students will be able to collaborate with other students to systematically problem solve, using statistics and research while factoring in environmental and economic issues of a region outside of their community.

DURATION

Two class periods for videoconferences.

Three class periods for other activities.

PRIOR KNOWLEDGE REQUIRED

Students should have an understanding of

- the coal industry in southern Ohio, and its current state;
- the effects sulfur has on the environment;
- the changing states of matter; and
- environmental, physical, political, and topographical maps.

VOCABULARY

Introduce the following words through this lesson:

acid mine drainage
aquatic ecosystem
conservancy
dredging
ecosystem
erosion
hydrogen sulfide
hydrogen sulfide gas
reservoir
sedimentation
strip mining
sulfur
Surface Mining Control and Reclamation Act of 1977
watershed

RESOURCES

Although this lesson plan focuses on water conservancy issues in Ohio, there are many regional water conservancy resource programs across the United States. This lesson may be easily adapted using the resources of your local water conservancy agencies. Here are some helpful links:

Regional education projects
www.awwa.org/waterwiser/education/casestudies.cfm

Natural Resources Conservation Services (Department of Agriculture)
www.wcc.nrcs.usda.gov/wetdrain/

Watershed Rehabilitation Information
www.nrcs.usda.gov/programs/WSRehab/

USGS Water Resources of the U.S.
http://water.usgs.gov

Pre-Conference Activities

Activity 1 • Understanding Maps

Instructional Objective

Students are able to use environmental, physical, political, and topographical maps to locate Ohio's reservoirs and the streams that reduce water tables. Students are able to identify the flow of water and determine which reservoirs support a given community.

Materials

- Environmental map of Ohio listing lakes, streams, and parks
- Physical map of Ohio
- Physical map of Northeast Ohio, Northwest Ohio, Southwest Ohio, or Southeast Ohio
- Political map of Ohio
- Political map of Northeast Ohio, Northwest Ohio, Southwest Ohio, or Southeast Ohio
- Topographical map of Northeast Ohio, Northwest Ohio, Southwest Ohio or Southeast Ohio
- Colored pencils or highlighters
- Student worksheet for students to list, categorize, and rank reservoirs and streams.

Procedure

1. Divide students into four groups (one for each region of the state).
2. Give each group a list of cities that have been determined to be in danger of flooding.
3. Have students locate their cities, the surrounding lakes, reservoirs, and waterways using environmental and political maps.
4. Using the topographical and physical maps have students color or highlight the support streams and mark the direction or flow of the water with arrows.
5. Using the student worksheet, have students categorize the supporting reservoirs and streams as input, output, or reservoir and rank them in order of importance to the given cities.

Evaluation

The rubric for the lesson evaluates knowledge of maps, identification of environmental and political sites, and the ability to work as a group.

Activity 2 • Overview of the Muskingum Watershed Conservancy District

Instructional Objective

Students gain a better understanding of the function of watersheds, the use of dams to control the flow of water, and the historical perspective of water damage in Southern Ohio.

Materials

- Videotape of the flood of 1913, by the Muskingum Watershed Conservancy District (MWCD)
- Information guide titled Troubled Waters: A National Call for Renewal
- Brochure titled The Idea Holds Water, an overview of the MWCD
- Political maps of Ohio
- Video fact guide worksheet
- Colored pencils and highlighters

Procedure

1. Students discuss the upcoming project, the schools involved, and the task involved. They are assigned the task to solve a problem involving the Muskingum Valley Region and the MWCD reservoirs.

2. Students watch the videotape (12 minutes) about the flood of 1913 and the creation of the Southern Ohio reservoirs to develop an understanding of their functions and their necessity to the area. During the video, students complete a fact guide worksheet that will assist them during the videoconference with engineers from the MWCD.

3. After the video is complete, students identify the Muskingum Valley and the MWCD regions, using political maps and the Idea Holds Water brochure. Students identify the regions with the largest populations and the reservoirs using highlighters and colored pencils.

4. At the completion of the activity, students are divided into their work groups for the project and complete the video fact sheet using the Troubled Waters information guide and the Idea Holds Water brochure.

Evaluation

The rubric for the evaluation of this activity will weight heavily on the completion of the video fact sheet. Students must demonstrate an understanding of the function of the MWCD and become familiar with the area that the problem solving activity will take place.

Preparation for Videoconference

- Overview behavioral expectations for students during videoconference.

- Create and display a sign noting school name and location.

- Develop student questions (be sure to write them out and review with class the procedure for interaction).

Videoconference One

Topic: *Troubled Waters—Problem-Based Learning Activity*

Content provider and participants: *Four high school biology classes and two engineers from the Muskingum Watershed Conservancy District (MWCD).*

Introduction

10 minutes prior to the program start: Video and audio checks with each of the sites.

Start time: Introduction of schools and engineers from MWCD.

Engineers describe their roles in the MWCD and give a short review of the conservancy's role in the Muskingum Valley. References are made to the video of the flood of 1913 and the Idea Holds Water and Troubled Waters brochures.

Activity and/or Presentation

(30 minutes)

Engineers from the MWCD make the students aware that as many as 180 coal mines sit upstream of the Muskingum lakes. Recent test of the streams and reservoirs have forced the MWCD to notify the Muskingum Valley that acid mine drainage, sulfur, and other pollutants have been identified as entering the basin's rivers, streams and reservoirs, severely damaging the aquatic ecosystem.

Students are given the statistics involving water tests conducted throughout the Muskingum Valley, lists of the affected lakes and reservoirs, photos of affected areas, and the current state of the mining industry. Using hard copies of the data and Internet links, students research acid mine drainage and hydrogen sulfide and their effects on the environment. Students use their maps in groups to identify the affected areas.

Engineers from MWCD inform students that each group must research the problem and develop a solution to present to the connecting sites the following week.

Question/Answer or Discussion

(10–15 minutes)

Engineers from MWCD call on each site and group for specific questions about the lakes and the testing data as they relate to the problem. All sites are encouraged to place their microphones on privacy while the other sites ask and answer questions.

Videoconference Two

Topic: *Troubled Waters Presentations—Problem-Based Learning Activity*

Content Provider and participants: *Four high school biology classes and two engineers from the Muskingum Watershed Conservancy District (MWCD).*

Introduction

10 minutes prior to the program start: Video and audio checks with each of the sites.

Start time: Introduction of schools and engineers from MWCD.

Program overview and presentation procedure.

The facilitator reminds all participants that, due to time constraints and to encourage discussion between the sites and the MWCD staff, there will be only one presentation per site.

Activity and/or Presentation

(30 minutes)

The project facilitator calls on each of the connecting sites to give their presentations on their solution to the problem.

Each class has 10 minutes to present its solution to the acid mine drainage. Students can use video broadcasts, presentation software, and images on the document camera for visual aides.

Once the group has been completed, the engineers from MWCD ask questions of the group for clarification and make positive comments. The engineers also discuss the effects the proposals have on the surrounding environments (positive/negative). The engineers call the next school for the next presentation.

Question/Answer or Discussion

(10–15 minutes)

When the presentations are completed, classes are encouraged to ask each other questions on research data, presentation strategies, and problem-solving strategies.

Facilitators with time remaining take turns connecting to the schools to discuss the positives and negatives of the project from the students' points of view.

Post-Conference Activities

Follow-up Activity • Compare and Contrast Presentations

Instructional Objective

Students gain a better understanding of the group process and how different groups can come up with multiple solutions to the same problem.

Materials

- Project website
- Internet worksheet

Procedure

Students post a narrative summary of their project to a discussion board. Each student posts a comment to the posting of another group. Each student completes a worksheet that summarizes a project completed by another group at his/her school and a project posted by another school.

Evaluation

The evaluation is based on the students' posting to the discussion board. The rubric for the posting activity weighs the data collected from the other groups' postings on the Internet worksheet and the posting to the discussion board.

Social Studies

Cotton, Plant of Many Uses

THELIA LISLE
Stamford High School, Stamford, Texas

TYPE OF LESSON:	*Student-Created Content*
GRADE LEVEL:	*10–12*

The Evolution of Video Applications in Distance Education

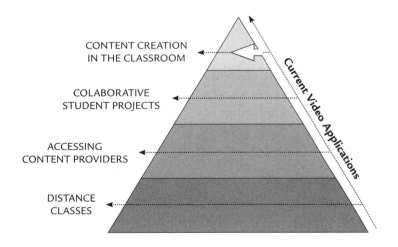

CORRELATION TO STANDARDS

ISTE NETS for Students

This lesson plan correlates to all of the NETS•S. For a complete list of the standards, please see Appendix B.

UNIT GOAL

To be able use various technology skills to create an instructional unit for elementary students and then conduct a live, interactive presentation of the lesson through distance-learning channels. Students research and create pre-conference learning activities for elementary students to correlate with the lesson's objectives.

LESSON OBJECTIVES

After completing this lesson, students will be able to

- create an instructional website;
- create downloadable student activities;
- shoot and edit a video;
- demonstrate presentation skills by conducting an interactive conference with elementary students; and
- manipulate ITV equipment, including document camera, microphone, DVD player, and instructor camera and various pre-sets.

DURATION

This depends on the depth of the lesson undertaken. Creating the website and all the activities and videos took about a semester. We continually update it and try to improve on the quality of our activities and presentation.

PRIOR KNOWLEDGE REQUIRED

Students should have an understanding of

- software applications and saving in interchangeable formats such as PDF or RTF,
- video capture and editing,
- audio capture and editing, and
- web authoring.

VOCABULARY

Words to be introduced through this lesson:

accessibility issues
curriculum standards
target audience
universal formats
usability issues

Overview

When we first developed our project, we beta-tested it with as many elementary classes as possible. We contacted schools and asked if they would participate with us in helping us refine our project. After each presentation, we asked teachers to fill out the evaluation form we have on our website and return it to us. We used that information to fine-tune our presentation.

The first objective when undertaking a project of this magnitude is to brainstorm with students about topics:

- What are the interests of elementary school students?
- Can this topic be used in a multidisciplinary lesson?
- Is it expandable for future use?
- Will it be engaging to elementary school students and hold their interest for a 30–45 minute conference presentation?
- Does the topic lend itself to hands-on, interactive activities for the day of the conference?
- Are sufficient resources available for this topic?
- Can this topic be presented in a variety of visual and auditory styles?

The second objective is to decide the target age of the audience.

Once these objectives are accomplished, the content of the project should be divided among groups of students for the purpose of researching facts and data that can be used. For instance, in our project we decided to tie geography, history, and science curriculum standards to our lesson, so we divided into three groups. Each group had to research the national educational standards for their curriculum area and locate standards that could be addressed in our project. Each group also had to identify student objectives for their curriculum area and create some age-appropriate activities that addressed those standards.

Once the teacher resources are completed and added to the Cotton: Plant of Many Uses website, students turn their attention to preparing for the videoconferences themselves.

This lesson is based on the project "Cotton, Plant of Many Uses," which can be viewed at www2.stamford.esc14.net:1090/.

Pre-Conference Activities

Activity 1 • Cotton Plants

Instructional Objective

To produce a video that shows cotton actively growing in a field and explains the science of the life cycle of the cotton plant and how cotton is ultimately harvested.

Materials

- Video camera
- Microphone

Procedure

Have students write a script that contains all the information that needs to be conveyed by the video. Talk about using appropriate hand gestures to present material and taking video shots to accompany the script. Have students create a storyboard for the video project that provides a plan for the shots and timing. Students then shoot the video following the script and storyboards. When filming on site, conditions may not be optimal for sound recording. It may be necessary do a voice-over audio and edit the video to match.

Evaluation

Review the video and instruct students to edit it as necessary.

Activity 2 • Cotton Gin

Instructional Objective

To create a hands-on activity that engages the elementary school–aged audience and helps them better understand the importance of the invention of the cotton gin.

Materials

- Cotton bolls (enough for each remote participant to have one), mailed to the remote site in advance of the presentation date.
- Various cotton by-products (fabric, cotton seed, animal feed, cotton swabs, cotton balls).

Procedure

Use the document camera with picture-in-picture (PIP) for this part. Have the remote teacher distribute cotton bolls to each student. Using the document camera, identify the parts of the cotton boll and explain their purposes. Have students pull out a single lock of fiber from their boll and feel for the seeds. Have the students extract a single seed, keeping the rest of the cotton fiber intact. Talk about the difficulty of doing this and how long it takes to hand pick all the cotton shown in the video and then hand pull the locks out and extract each seed without harming the remaining fiber. This hands-on activity demonstrates the importance of the cotton gin and how it revolutionized the cotton industry.

Student shows cotton boll using document camera

Preparation for Videoconference

About two weeks before the conference, mail a box with the cotton bolls and cotton by-products in it to the participating schools.

Remote-site students should complete the Geography Unit—Student Activity Worksheet 1 (downloaded from the website), in which they identify and label cotton-belt states. Students should have these maps available during the videoconference.

Ask the teachers to allow their students to go to our website and familiarize themselves with our students. We have a students' page linked to our cotton site, where we include photos of the students participating in this year's cotton project, along with a short introduction of themselves and our town. Our goal is to develop a relationship with the remote-site students so that they feel more comfortable talking to us on the day of our presentation. We ask them to plan out some questions about cotton or our students or our school to ask us on the day of our connection.

Interaction is key to success. Have students identify students at remote sites individually, for example, by saying things like, "Can the boy in the front row with the yellow shirt tell me...?"). This personalizes it more. At the beginning of our conference, my students always introduce themselves and tell a little bit about themselves individually. We try to make a connection between the "presenter" students and the "audience" students.

Videoconference

Topic: *Cotton, Plant of Many Uses*

Content Provider: *Stamford High School Technology Students*

Activity and/or Presentation

Students take turns being responsible for presenting each segment. All segments are supported by student activities that are to be completed prior to the day of the conference.

The geography of cotton. Talk about the cotton-belt states and ask students to show the Geography Unit—Student Activity Worksheet 1 maps they completed previous to the videoconference. Talk about why cotton is only grown in these states.

Cotton products. Using the document camera, talk about the various by-products sent in the mail and how each relates to cotton.

Video. Show the video created in Activity 1—Cotton Plants.

Cotton bolls. Using the document camera, identify the parts of the boll. Have students identify the parts on their individual cotton bolls. Have them remove a lock of the cotton and find the seeds. Have them remove individual seeds, keeping the cotton fiber intact. This leads into the discussion of the cotton gin.

History of the cotton gin. Talk about the invention and show a diagram on the document camera of how the early concept of the cotton gin worked.

History. Talk about how cotton came to the United States and what obstacles the cotton industry had to overcome, illustrating with pictures shown on the document camera.

Give an overview of cotton's importance to the Confederacy during the Civil War, again using pictures shown on the document camera to illustrate. Use the cotton belt map to identify the states that seceded from the Union, and talk about how cotton impacted the outcome of the Civil War.

Cotton processing. In this segment, talk about the processes that cotton goes through as it moves from field to fabric, using the document camera to show pictures that illustrate the processes.

Importance of cotton products. In this segment, talk about the various job opportunities related to cotton and tell how many other industries are supported and impacted by cotton. Use the document camera to show pictures to illustrate all of these jobs and industries.

Cotton Gin Video. We shot a video at our local cotton gin and had the gin manager take us through and explain all of the various machines and processes within the gin. This video is narrated by the gin manager and shows a working gin and the components inside and shows the process from cotton module (from the field) to the cotton bales that are shipped around the world.

Students present a segment during the videoconference

Question/Answer or Discussion

(10–15 minutes)

The last part of the videoconference is for questions from the remote-site students. Our students take turns answering questions and asking them questions.

Provide directions for how this interaction will take place. For example, who will ask the leading question, who will respond, how long does each student have to ask a question or respond to a question, and so forth.

Ask the remote-site teacher to help facilitate this by calling on their students and asking them to stand up and ask the question. We have a Procedural Suggestions for the Day of the Virtual Field Trip section on our website with suggestions to help facilitate the flow of the live presentation.

Post-Conference Activities

Follow-up Activity

Instructional Objective

To review and reinforce facts and information learned in the cotton unit through the various activities and the live presentation.

Procedure

Create a "Jeopardy" game in PowerPoint for teachers to use post-conference as a fun way to follow up on the knowledge students gained from the cotton unit.

Chapter 5

Instructional
Resources
for
Videoconference Lessons

This chapter is a compilation of resources to assist you in planning your own interactive videoconference-empowered lessons. It includes

- **Videoconference Lesson Plan Template:** a lesson plan template that was used by all the teachers who contributed to this book;

- **Student Evaluation of IVC Lesson:** a sample student evaluation form that may be adapted to fit the needs of your students; and

- **Online Resources:** a collection of the best of the best in online resources that will enable you to quickly find the content, collaborative partners, and projects that you need.

Videoconference Lesson Plan Template

GRADE LEVEL

CORRELATION TO STANDARDS

(This section should show the alignment of the lesson plan objectives with state and national benchmarks and standards.)

UNIT GOAL

LESSON OBJECTIVES

After completing this lesson, the students will be able to:
(list the objectives)

DURATION

(Indicate the period of time this lesson plan is taught, for example, "Three to four class periods.")

PRIOR KNOWLEDGE REQUIRED

Students should have an understanding of: (list the requirements)

VOCABULARY

Words to be introduced through this lesson: (list the words and terms)

Pre-Conference Activities

Activity 1

Instructional Objective

Materials

Procedure

Evaluation

Activity 2

Instructional Objective

Materials

Procedure

Evaluation

Preparation for Videoconference

- Review expectations for behavior during videoconference.
- Create and display a sign noting school name and location.
- Develop student questions to be asked; write them out and review with class the procedure for interaction.

Videoconference

Topic:

Content provider (or remote site):

Introduction

Activity and/or Presentation

Question/Answer or Discussion

10–15 minutes (for example).

(Provide directions for how this interaction will take place: who will ask the leading question, who will respond, how long each student has to ask a question or respond to a question, and so forth.)

Post-Conference Activities

Follow-up Activity

Instructional Objective

Materials

Procedure

Evaluation

Student Evaluation of IVC Lesson

GRADE LEVEL: _____

SUBJECT/TEACHER: _____

DATE OF IVC: _____

TIME OF IVC: _____

Rate the following statements from (1) strongly disagree, to (4) strongly agree.

STATEMENT	1	2	3	4
This is the first videoconference I have participated in this year.				
The videoconference was in addition to the lesson my teacher was teaching.				
The videoconference was a part of the lesson my teacher was teaching.				
The presenter was easy to understand and communicate with during the videoconference.				
The presenter offered a question and answer time at the end of the videoconference.				
Pre-videoconference activities supported the content delivered.				
Activities during the videoconference supported the lesson we were doing in class.				
Post-videoconference activities supported the content delivered during the videoconference.				
I will use information learned from the videoconference when I take the test over this lesson.				
I learned something from the videoconference that I did not know before.				
Everyone in my class paid attention to the presenter during the videoconference.				
More than one classroom participated in the videoconference.				
My teacher was in charge of the videoconference.				
The remote location was in charge of the videoconference.				
Using videoconferencing technology made the lesson more interesting to me.				

Online Resources

Content Resources

CILC—Center for Interactive Learning and Collaboration

www.cilc.org

> This is the major clearinghouse for interactive videoconferencing content. You can search by topic, price, standards, and grade level. This site features the most up-to-date virtual fieldtrips, including national standards and teacher evaluations.

Connect 2 Texas

www.connect2texas.net

> The purpose of this site is to promote programs offered by interactive videoconferencing providers in Texas. It is also for the use of schools and other entities to register for programs given by one of their Texas providers.

EEZ—Education Enterprise Zone

www.nyiteez.org

> Hosted by the New York Institute of Technology, the EEZ site features offerings from content providers mainly in the northeastern United States, but some are from across the country. This site features an online community and a downloadable book about best practices in educational videoconferencing.

TWICE—Two Way Interactive Connections in Education

www.twice.cc/

> K–12 content is found on this site. There are hundreds of programs for interactive video lessons. The TWICE site features field trips, shared classes, and collaborative projects.

Collaborative Resources

ATT Knowledge Network

www.kn.att.com/wired/vidconf/vidconf.html

> This site has been around for many years. It features a content directory to aid in searches for content providers and end-users in the K–12 educational community. It also is the home of the Ed1Vid Con e-mail list, a huge list that one can subscribe to in order to receive postings covering IVC events, new content offerings, and collaborative project offerings.

CILC Collaborative Portal

www.cilc.org/c/community/collaboration_center.aspx

> Visit this web page to search projects, post your own project idea to find partners, or browse collaborative project ideas from teachers around the world. It is updated on a regular basis.

Collaborative Projects with Videoconferencing Wiki

http://collaborativevcs.pbwiki.com

> Collaborative Projects with Videoconferencing Wiki is managed by Berrien County Independent School District in Michigan. View collaborative projects posted by educators in every discipline. Post your own project. Links to archived projects, too.

MAGPI K20 Programs

www.magpi.net/programs/index.html

> Targeted toward schools that are Internet2 enabled, MAGPI offers various collaborative projects throughout the school year in every subject area.

Global Projects

Global Run

www.globalrunproject.org

> A yearly, ongoing project that connects schools around the globe for working together on a topic of world concern. Global Run grows larger each year, and the best way to learn about it is to view the videos found on their web page.

iEARN

www.iearn.org

> Started in 1988, iEARN is the world's largest nonprofit global network that enables teachers and young people to use the Internet and other new technologies to collaborate on projects that both enhance learning and make a difference in the world.

Megaconference Jr.

www.megaconferencejr.org

> Megaconference Jr., now in its sixth year, is a project designed to give students in elementary and secondary schools around the world the opportunity to communicate, collaborate, and contribute to each other's learning in real time using advanced, multi-point, videoconferencing technology. Megaconference Jr. is a one-day event that takes place in early spring and is modeled on its predecessor, Megaconference, a similar event for Internet2 higher education members.

IVC Blogs

Avon, Ohio's Interactive Video Distance Learning Blog

http://avonoh-ivc.blogspot.com

> This blog is an electric diary of the Avon Local Schools' Distance Learning Project maintained by Paul Hieronymus, also author of the high school science lesson in this book. Postings go back to September 2005.

Videoconference Tips and Techniques

http://videoconference.edublogs.org

> From Carol Daunt in Australia, this blog has lots of how-to tips for educators and trainers. It includes frequent postings dating from April 2006.

Videoconferencing Out on a Lim

http://bcisdvcs.wordpress.com

> This is a blog dedicated to the latest news in IVC for K–12 schools. Maintained by Janine Lim of Berrien County ISD in Michigan, the blog also has links to other blogs of interest to this community.

The Wired Classroom

http://csdtechpd.wordpress.com

> The Cooperating School Districts' Virtual Learning Center Blog is an active blog on videoconferencing in K–12. Originating in St. Louis, Missouri, it includes postings that start June 2006.

Got Videoconferencing?

http://gotvideoconferencing.blogspot.com

> This website has postings from Andrea Israeli of Queens, New York. Since January 2006 she has been posting entries about videoconferencing projects her students have been involved with.

General Resources

MAGPI

www.magpi.net/vcresources.html

> H323 Videoconferencing Resources from MAGPI is a collection of links to other sites, as well as how-to tips concerning collaborative projects, technical information, and information about Internet2 initiatives.

References and Resources

References

Cole, C., Ray, K., & Zanetis, J. (2009). *Videoconferencing for K–12 classrooms, second edition*. Eugene, OR: International Society for Technology in Education.

Davis, D. & Edyburn, D. (2007, February). Naked independence vs. performance support. *Learning & Leading with Technology, 34*(5), 8–9.

Marcel, K. W. (2004, December). *Using technology to increase access to accelerated learning opportunities in four states* (Document No. 2A353). Boulder, CO: Western Interstate Commission for Higher Education.

National Research Council (2001). *Educating teachers of science, mathematics, and technology*. Washington, DC: National Academy Press.

National Research Council. (2002). In J. D. Bransford, A. L. Brown, & R. R. Cocking (Eds.), *How people learn: Brain, mind, experience and school* (expanded edition). Washington, DC: National Academy Press.

November, A. (2001). *Empowering students with technology*. Arlington Heights, IL: SkyLight Professional Development.

Pflaum, W. (2004). The technology fix: *The promise and reality of computers in our schools*. Alexandria, VA: Association for Supervision and Curriculum Development.

U.S. Department of Education (2004). *Toward a new golden age in American education: How the Internet, the law and today's students are revolutionizing expectations*. Washington, DC: U.S. Government Printing Office. Retrieved from www.nationaledtechplan.org

Resources

Aleksic-Maslac, K., & Jeren, B. (2001, August). Asynchronous distance learning model. *International conference on engineering education* (pp. 13-16). Oslo, Norway: International Conference on Engineering Education.

Amirian, S. (2003, October). Pedagogy & videoconferencing: A review of recent literature. A poster session presentation at NJEDge.NET Conference, Plainsboro, NJ.

Anderson, L. W., & Krathwohl (Eds.). (2001). A taxonomy for learning, teaching, and assessing: A revision of Bloom's Taxonomy of Educational Objectives. New York: Longman.

AYA/ELA (2004). Candidate guide to national board certification. Retrieved January 5, 2004, from www.nbpts.org/candidates/guide/04port/04_ayaela_instructions/04_aya_ela_resources.pdf

Baker, M. (January, 2007). Moving pictures are on the move. *Distance Learning Today*, pp. 8, 15. Available from www.dltoday.net/_pdf/issue01.pdf

Bigham, S., Kellogg, J., & Hodges, J. (Eds.). (1995). *Telecommunications technology planning manual*. Nashville, TN: South Central Bell.

Blank, M. (1999). Everything you ever wanted to know about H.323. *Teleconferencing Magazine*. Retrieved October 25, 2003, from www.teleconferencemagazine.com

Branzburg, J. (2001). Videoconferencing? *Technology & Learning, 22*(2), 54–57.

Budniewski, D. (2003, October 23). DEVO take UB classroom to the global community. *University at Buffalo Reporter, 35*(9). Retrieved April 16, 2004, from http://people.uis.edu/rschr1/onlinelearning/archive/2003_10_19_archive.html

Caine, R. N., & Caine, G. (1994). Making connections: teaching and the human brain. New York: Addison-Wesley.

Cashman, S. (2003). *Discovering computers: A gateway to information.* Boston: Course Technology.

Cavanaugh, C. S. (2001). The effectiveness of interactive distance education technologies in K–12 learning: A meta-analysis. *International Journal of Educational Telecommunications, 7*(1), 73–88.

Clark, T. (2001). *Virtual schools: Trends and issues. A study of virtual schools in the United States.* Phoenix, AZ: Distance Learning Resource Network at WestEd. Retrieved October 18, 2002, from www.wested.org/online_pubs/virtualschools.pdf

Cole, C., Ray, K., & Zanetis, J. (2004). *Videoconferencing for K–12 classrooms: A program development guide.* Eugene, OR: International Society for Technology in Education.

Crews, K. (2003, April 8). New copyright law for distance education: The meaning and importance of the TEACH Act. Article prepared for the American Library Association. Chicago: American Library Association.

Dede, C. (1996). Emerging technologies and distributed learning. *The American Journal of Distance Education, 10*(2), 4–36.

deFord, K., & Dimock, V. (2002, June). Understanding the value of interactive videoconferencing technology in improving K–12 educational systems: Vol. 1. *Interactive Videoconferencing: A Policy Issues Review, 1–7.* A Regional Technology in Education Consortia National Collaborative Project. Washington DC: Regional Technology in Education Consortia.

The Digital Millennium Act of 1998, Pub. L. No. 105–304, 112 Stat. 2860 (1998).

Foshee, D. (1997). Planning the smart classroom: A practical primer for designing interactive video learning environments. Austin, TX: VTel Corp.

Goldberg, L. (2002, March 20). Our technology future. *Education Week, 21*(27), 32, 34. Retrieved November 13, 2003, from www.edweek.org/ew/newstory.cfm?slug=27goldberg.h21

Gonzales, A. H., & Nelson, L. M. (2005, January). Learner-Centered Instruction Promotes Student Success. *THE Journal Online.* Retrieved January 21, 2005, from www.thejournal.com.

Green, K. (2003, December). Tracking the digital puck into 2004. *Syllabus Magazine,* Retrieved November 13, 2003, from www.syllabus.com/article.asp?id=8574

Hanor, J., & Hayden, K. *Improving learning for all students through technology [ILAST].* Abstract retrieved November 10, 2003, from www.ilast.org

Hanson, D., Maushak, N., Scholosser, C., Anderson, M., Sorensen, C., & Simonson, M. (1997). *Distance education: Review of the literature.* Bloomington, Indiana: Association for Educational Communications & Technology.

Hayden, K. (1999). Videoconferencing in K–12 Education: A Delphi study of characteristics and critical strategies to support constructivist learning experiences. (Doctoral dissertation, Pepperdine University, 1999). *Dissertation Abstract International, 60, 06A.*

Heath, M. (1997). *The design, development, and implementation of a virtual online classroom.* Unpublished dissertation. University of Houston, Texas.

Heath, M., & Holznagel, D. (2002, June). Understanding the value of interactive videoconferencing technology: Vol. 1. Interactive videoconferencing: A literature review. A Regional Technology in Education Consortia National Collaborative Project. Washington DC: Regional Technology in Education Consortia.

Holznagel, D. C. (2003). *Access and opportunity, policy options for interactive video in K–12 education.* Portland, OR: Northwest Regional Educational Laboratory.

Holznagel, D. C. (2003, June). Access and Opportunity: Policy Options for Interactive Video in K–12 Education. Symposium conducted at the meeting of the Regional Educational Laboratory and Educational Technology Consortium Practitioners, Dallas, Texas.

Hopkins, G. L. (1995). *The ISDN literacy book.* New York: Addison-Wesley.

Huitt, W. (2004). In Bloom et al's *Taxonomy of the Cognitive Domain.* Retrieved April 23, 2005, from http://chiron.valdosta.edu/whuitt/col/cogxyx/bloom.html

Interactive videoconferencing in K–12 settings. (2002, October). Regional Technology in Education Consortia paper presented at A Symposium for Practitioners, Dallas, Texas.

Johnstone, S. M., & Witherspoon, J. P. (2001, March). *Quality in online education: Results from a revolution [Special issue]*. 15(3), Retrieved on May 12, 2002 from www.usdla.org/ED_magazine/illuminactive/MAR01_Issue/index.html

Kent School District. (n.d.). Teaching Using Blooms Taxonomy, Retrieved April 23, 05, from www.kent.k12.wa.us

Kerca, S. (1996). *Distance learning, the Internet, and the World Wide Web.* East Lansing, MI: National Center for Research on Teacher Learning. ERIC Document Reproduction Service No. ED395214.

Kober, N. (1990). Think rural means isolated? Not when distance learning reaches into school. *The School Administrator, 47*(10), 16–24.

Kozma, R. B. (2003). A review of the findings and their implications for practice and plocu. In R. Kozma (Ed.), *Technology, innovation, and educational change: A global perspective.* Eugene, OR: International Society for Educational Technology.

Krell, E. Videoconferencing gets the call. *Training.* Retrieved August 2, 2002, from Proquest, an online information service: www.vanderbilt.edu/library

Kuralt, C. (1990). *A life on the road.* New York: G. P. Putnam's Sons.

Kvaternik, R. (2002). *Teacher education guidelines: Using open and distance learning.* Paris: UNESCO.

Lockett, E., & Strode-Penny, L. (1998, September 24, 25). Child studies educational videoconferencing. Paper presented at Learning Technologies '98, Queensland, Australia.

McKenzie, J. (2003). Pedagogy does matter. *The Ed Tech Journal, 13*(1.1), 2. Retrieved December 16, 2003, from www.fno.org/sept03/pedagogy.html

Merriam-Webster [Dictionary]. Merriam-Webster Online. Retrieved January 3, 2004, from www.merriam-Webster.com

Moore, M. G. (1991). Theory of distance education [Monograph]. University Park, PA: American Center for the Study of Distance Education.

Moore, M. G. (1993). Theory of transactional distance. In D. Keegan (Ed.), *Theoretical principles of distance education* (pp. 22–37). London, New York: Routledge.

Moore, M. G., & Kearsley, G. (1996). *Distance education: A systems view.* Boston: Wadsworth.

Muilenburg, L., S. & Berge, Z. (2001). Barriers of distance education: A factor analytic study. *The American Journal of Distance Education, 15*(2), 7–24.

Mullane, J., & Cataline, J. (2002, Spring). Harness the power of videoconferencing through ongoing support. *FETC Connections, 1, 6–7.*

National Research Council. (2002). J. D. Bransford, A. L. Brown, & R. R. Cocking (Eds.), *How people learn: Brain, mind, experience and school* (Expanded edition). Washington DC: National Academy Press.

National Science Teachers Association (May, 2007). The state of teaching with technology, *NSTA Reports, 18*(9), 1, 5

Negroponte, N., Resnick, M., & Cassell, J. (n.d.). *Creating a learning revolution.* Abstract retrieved August 29, 2002, from www.unesco.org/education/educprog/lwf/doc/protfolio/opinion8.htm

The No Child Left Behind Act of 2001, Pub. L. No. 107–110, 115 Stat. 1426 (2002).

North Central Regional Educational Laboratory. (2003). *Indicator: Technology-ready facilities.* Abstract retrieved October 9, 2003, from www.ncrel.org/engauge/framewk/acc/facility/accfacra.htm

Northwest Educational Technology Consortium and Northwest Regional Educational Laboratory. (2000). Issues for K–12 decision makers. In *Digital bridges: Videoconferencing for teaching and learning.* Portland, Oregon: Northwest Educational Technology Consortium.

Northwest Educational Technology Consortium and Northwest Regional Educational Laboratory. (2000). Promising practices for K–12 videoconferencing. In *Digital bridges: Videoconferencing for teaching and learning.* Portland, Oregon: Northwest Education Technology Consortium.

November, A. (2001). *Empowering Students with Technology.* Arlington Heights, IL: SkyLight Professional Development.

Pachnowski, L. (2002). Virtual field trips through videoconferencing. *Learning & Leading with Technology, 29*(6), 12.

Ray, K. (2002). *A history of videoconferencing.* Unpublished manuscript, Vanderbilt University, Nashville, TN.

Ray, K. (2002, September). *Increasing science literacy through virtual connections* [Short paper/poster]. Presented at Conference on Ontological, Epistemological, Linguistic and Pedagogical Considerations of Language and Science Literacy: Empowering Research and Informing Instruction, Victoria, British Columbia, Canada.

Saba, F. (2003). *Distance education: A systems approach.* PDF file available from www.distance-educator.com/k12/

Sadker, M., & Sadker, D. (1994). The history of American education. In *Teachers, schools, and society* (3rd ed.), pp. 102–103. New York: McGraw-Hill.

Shearer, R. L. (2003). Interaction in Distance Education. *Distance Educator Special Report 2*(1). Madison, WI: Atwood Publishing.

Sherry, L. (1996). Issues in distance learning. *International Journal of Educational Telecommunications, 1*(4), 337–365.

Sherry, L., & Morse, R. (1995). An assessment of training needs in the use of distance education for instruction. *International Journal of Educational Telecommunications, 1*(1), 5–22. Reprinted (1996, Winter) in *Educational Technology Review, 5,* 10–17.

Smyth, R. & Zanetis, J. (August, 2007). Internet-Based Videoconferencing for Teaching and Learning: A Cinderella Story. *Distance Learning, 4*(2), 61–70.

Specialist Schools Trust. (2000, July). *One world one school.* Paper presented at Vision 2020 Conference, Dartford, United Kingdom. Retrieved January 11, 2004, from www.schoolsnetwork.org.uk

Sueoka, L. (April, 2007). Cyber humanities: rigor and relevance through videoconferencing. *Learning & Leading with Technology, 34*(7) 28–30.

Sullivan, M., Jolly, D., Foster, D., & Tompkins, R. (1994). *Local heroes: A guidebook for bringing telecommunications to rural, small schools.* Austin, TX: Southwest Educational Development Laboratory.

Tapscott, D. (1998). *Growing up digital.* New York: McGraw Hill.

Tapscott, D. (1998). *The net generation and the school.* Retrieved November 10, 2000, from the Milken Exchange on Education Technology website: www.mff.org

Tucker, P.D., & Stronge, J. H. (2005). *Linking teacher evaluation and student learning.* Alexandria: ASCD.

UNESCO. (1997). *World communications report: The media and the challenges of the new technologies.* Paris: Author.

UNESCO. (1998a). *World education report 1998: Teachers and teaching in a changing world* (Summary), Paris: Author. Available from www.unesco.org/education/educprog/wer/wer.htm

UNESCO (1998b). *Creating learning networks for African teachers.* Available from www.unesco.org/education /unesco/educprog/lwf/doc/IA1.html

UNESCO Education News. (1998, September/November). Ambitious plan for teachers. *Copy Editor, 14,* 1–2. Available from www.unesco.org/education/educnews/sept/cd14.pdf

U.S. Department of Education, National Center for Educational Statistics. (2001). *Internet access in U. S. public schools: 1994–2000,* by Anne Cattagni and Elizabeth Farris. (NCES 2001–071). Washington, DC: U. S. Government Printing Office.

U.S. Department of Education, National Center for Education Statistics. (2002). *A profile of participation in distance education, 1999–2000,* by Anna C. Sikora. (NCES 2003–154). Washington, DC: U. S. Government Printing Office.

Vincent, J. (2003). Individual difference, technology and the teacher of the future. In Australian Computer Society, Inc. Melbourne, Australia: IFIP Working Groups 3.1 and 3.3 Working Group Conference.

The Ward Melville Heritage Organization. (2002, March). Videoconferencing exposes students to new worlds. *T.H.E. Journal Online,* Retrieved June 7, 2002, from www.thejournal.com/magazine/vault/A3945C.fm?kw=719

Weigel, V. B. (2002). *Deep learning for a digital age: Technology's untapped potential to enrich higher education.* New York: Jossey-Bass.

National Educational Technology Standards for Students (NETS•S)

All K–12 students should be prepared to meet the following standards and performance indicators.

1. **Creativity and Innovation**

   Students demonstrate creative thinking, construct knowledge, and develop innovative products and processes using technology. Students:

   a. apply existing knowledge to generate new ideas, products, or processes

   b. create original works as a means of personal or group expression

   c. use models and simulations to explore complex systems and issues

   d. identify trends and forecast possibilities

2. **Communication and Collaboration**

   Students use digital media and environments to communicate and work collaboratively, including at a distance, to support individual learning and contribute to the learning of others. Students:

   a. interact, collaborate, and publish with peers, experts, or others employing a variety of digital environments and media

   b. communicate information and ideas effectively to multiple audiences using a variety of media and formats

   c. develop cultural understanding and global awareness by engaging with learners of other cultures

   d. contribute to project teams to produce original works or solve problems

3. **Research and Information Fluency**
   Students apply digital tools to gather, evaluate, and use information. Students:

   a. plan strategies to guide inquiry

   b. locate, organize, analyze, evaluate, synthesize, and ethically use information from a variety of sources and media

   c. evaluate and select information sources and digital tools based on the appropriateness to specific tasks

   d. process data and report results

4. **Critical Thinking, Problem Solving, and Decision Making**
   Students use critical-thinking skills to plan and conduct research, manage projects, solve problems, and make informed decisions using appropriate digital tools and resources. Students:

   a. identify and define authentic problems and significant questions for investigation

   b. plan and manage activities to develop a solution or complete a project

   c. collect and analyze data to identify solutions and make informed decisions

   d. use multiple processes and diverse perspectives to explore alternative solutions

5. **Digital Citizenship**
   Students understand human, cultural, and societal issues related to technology and practice legal and ethical behavior. Students:

   a. advocate and practice the safe, legal, and responsible use of information and technology

   b. exhibit a positive attitude toward using technology that supports collaboration, learning, and productivity

   c. demonstrate personal responsibility for lifelong learning

   d. exhibit leadership for digital citizenship

6. **Technology Operations and Concepts**
   Students demonstrate a sound understanding of technology concepts, systems, and operations. Students:

   a. understand and use technology systems

   b. select and use applications effectively and productively

   c. troubleshoot systems and applications

   d. transfer current knowledge to the learning of new technologies